Dream Catcher 52

Stairwell Books //

Dream Catcher 52

SUBSCRIPTIONS TO DREAM CATCHER MAGAZINE

£18.00 UK (Two issues inc. p&p)
£25.00 Europe
£28.00 USA and Canada

Cheques should be made
payable to **Dream Catcher**
and sent to:

Dream Catcher Subscriptions
161 Lowther Street
York, YO31 7LZ
UK

+44 1904 733767

argillott@gmail.com

www.dreamcatchermagazine.co.uk
@literaryartsmag
www.stairwellbooks.co.uk
@stairwellbooks

Dream Catcher Magazine

Dream Catcher No. 52

ISSN: 1466-9455

Published by Stairwell Books //

ISBN: 978-1-917334-31-0

York UNESCO
City of Media Arts

Contents – Authors

FEATURED ARTIST
ARTIST STATEMENT: JOSEPH BUCKLOW

Using imagination, memory and photography as sources of inspiration, Bucklow's paintings capture landscapes, urban scenes and the people within them imbued with a stark drama. The images tend to be brooding, half-seen poetic visions that blur the lines between nostalgia and history, theatre and reality. These semi-imagined settings loom like light within a dream, offering a glimpse into worlds that are at once familiar and unknown. The work evokes a faded recollection, and the fragmented pleasure that can come with that, but also the unease and dynamism of the unexplored, providing enough visual information for the viewer to find their bearings whilst simultaneously surrendering to uncertainty and questioning. Rather than slavishly mimic a scene or compete with the camera lens, Bucklow lasers in on the intersection between certitude and recall, that flitting convergence between the definite and the question.

Wordworth defined poetry as , "the spontaneous overflow of powerful feelings: it takes its origin from emotion recollected in tranquility." For Bucklow, it's not the emotion or the recollection of it, but the painterly slippage between the two that inculcates his creativity with a David Lynch-esque chiaroscuro. Poet David Lewis Paget, in his 2005 poem 'Half Remembered' guides us through memories as if he is observing a previous life, 'another life's colours':

> "We touch things we see not
> And know things we know not
> And dream of sweet things that
> We've not set in store.
> We say things we think not
> And do things we do not
> And wonder at wonders
> We've wondered before…"

It is this yearning surrealism in revisiting reminiscences that Bucklow's paintings strive for: inaccuracy, enhancement and exaggerations, all products of selective memories, all providing subject matter for paintings that pulse with gestural brushwork and ligne claire, experimental wit and claustrophobic foreboding, expressing with Hitchcockian theatricality the notion that though what we remember is, like Ozymandias' statue, transient, the memories themselves cling while we live.

Greg McGee

PAGES OF ARTWORK

My conversation with Katrina Porteous invited reflection on how significant language is in articulating the identities and practices of particular cultures, and how the erosion or elimination of communities (be it through industrialisation, post industrialisation, or maybe climate change or other paradigm shift) can cause a real loss of 'voice'. Speech can be a 'marker of identity' – which in my experience can create a sense of alienation as well as belonging (after living in Yorkshire for thirty-six years I still get snide comments and assumptions made about me, based on my London accent). She also encouraged me to think anew about how poetry 'speaks' from beneath the radar – not just through conventional publication on a page (whether actual or digital) but through its function and context. Poems can shout from the side of buses; whisper from a well-worn bench; jostle the prayers and readings for a place in an order of service for a funeral. A friend of mine who does not read poetry recently asked me to define it, its boundaries with prose and all the other imponderables. Is a mass-produced rhyming ditty in a greetings card a poem? Is a dedication on a tombstone? We close this issue with another highly relevant question: what does it feel like to BE a poem?

This emphasis on loss and endings may sound rather valedictory; perhaps the increasingly short days of the northern hemisphere have infected my thinking. In DC 51 we had a record number of poems 'after' some other poet/phenomenon/artwork etc. The submissions this time seemed to be more dominated by sombre content, perhaps reflecting the increasingly fractured and fractious world we inhabit. Here, we say goodbye to loved ones; to youth; perhaps even to planet earth as Mars beckons. Sinister events await investigation in the graveyard; ladybirds invade the inner sanctum. Children's school days are punctuated by triage during warfare. Perhaps we are 'all cried out'.

But, as always, the brown envelopes that flopped onto my doormat also contained wit and warmth and wackiness. God clearly needs an assistant to complete the job (though are there enough women around to apply the Bechdel test to the book of Genesis?). A three year old relishes the mouthfeel of a new word. Spring and autumn love warm the cockles of the most jaded heart. At least, 'we very rarely eat our spouse'. And I'm also delighted to flag up the successes of poets whose work was shared through previous issues of Dream Catcher – new books are published or forthcoming by (among others), Emily Zobel Marshall, Elaine Ewart, Sue Butler, Philip Burton, Gerald Killingworth, Clive Donovan, Christopher James, Clifford Liles … we don't have space to review all the books suggested or sent to us, but it does create a warm glow to think that the community of writers – both poets and prose writers – whose work we are honoured to publish here are finding wider readership, that their voices are sustaining communities, breaking boundaries, holding things together. It's easy to find soundbites insisting that the task or role of writers is to do X or Y; but rather than capitulating to such a doctrinaire approach we could applaud writing as one of the last bastions of freedom.

Hannah Stone

HS: Katrina, thank you so much for agreeing to be my guest for this issue. I have been very struck by your work, having reviewed *Rhizodont* for *The Lake*, and as always with my guests I am especially interested in poets who have another string to their bow – and you evidently have several. Many poets draw on their heritage and lineage to provide substance and content for their poetry – can you say something about how your family connections to the north east, especially their working class lives, inform what you write about? I'm thinking about the first section of *Rhizodont* (Carboniferous) for example.

KP: With a few exceptions, the poems in *Rhizodont* are deliberately not 'personal'. The first section of *Rhizodont* is a journey along the coast of North East England from East Durham to the Scottish Border, a distance of about 60 miles, with which I have a lifelong connection. So my work does draw on my family heritage, although not usually in a direct way.

HS: I think that is an aspect of the work that really appeals to me – it is so much more than a veiled autobiography! Do tell me how you wove the heritage onto the weft of the concept.

KP: I didn't start with a concept. The book assembles a number of sequences of poems, written over several years, and the 'journey' suggested itself at a late stage. Putting a book together is rather like writing a poem, trying different combinations of parts to see how they resonate with one another and what arises from that. The title comes from the name of a fossil fish found near the Scottish Border in 2007. It lies in Carboniferous rock 330 million years old – the type of rock from which we have extracted fossil fuels like coal.

Many of us with roots in the North East have coal mining heritage. You're right that I've written extensively about working class lives, in inshore fishing as well as mining communities, and that does have an indirectly personal connection. I was born in Aberdeen, Scotland, to parents from North East England. My mother's father was a Durham miner and my father's parents retired to the Northumberland coast. The two sides of the family were very different from each other. When I was 7 we moved near to Consett, a Durham steel town on the edge of the Pennines, known for its clouds of red dust and its winter snowdrifts. For my parents this was a return home but for me, an only child, it was a displacement. As a 'foreigner' in primary school, I was physically bullied, and quickly learnt the power of speech as a marker of identity. I said 'barley' instead of 'skinch' (pax), 'piece' for a snack instead of 'bait'. My status as an outsider was about class as much as nationality. I was a doctor's daughter, so clearly not working class; but my mother's background gave me working class bones.

HS: That really resonates with me – my grandmother was a 'tweeny maid' (between a parlour maid and a scullery maid I believe) and my mother was the first in her family to stay on at school beyond minimum school leaving age and to go to university. My father was from very much more middle class roots. It can be a rich but sometimes conflicting situation?

KP: My mother came top of her class, but was denied grammar school because she was a girl. She left school at 15 to become a nurse. I'm acutely aware of the educational opportunities that I've enjoyed, which her family did not. I was close to my mother's family who remained in the pit village, and I still feel a deep attachment to those Durham coalfield communities and the exquisite countryside around them which I wrote about in *Two Countries* and to which I return in *Rhizodont*. For me that coalfield was a conflicted landscape and culture, industrial and rural, brutal and nurturing, and the closure of the collieries and subsequent restoration of that coast to an Area of Outstanding Natural Beauty has been similarly contradictory: both a miraculous recovery of nature and an enduring legacy of social deprivation.

HS: This explains how you appear as an 'adopted daughter' of the Northumbrian coast, an area I am especially fond of for its beauty, wildness, and sense of history, which I can only appreciate as a visitor. You have taken this immersion to a much deeper level, however, in absorbing and representing the dialect of the region to the extent that you are president of the Northumbrian Language Society. Can you tell us about this work, and how different types of English, mediated through location, are important to you?

KP: Although I always hoped to be a writer, I studied History, not English, at university. In 1987 I moved to my grandparents' house 60 miles north of Durham on the Northumberland coast, an area known for its castles, abbeys and earlier Anglo Saxon 'Golden Age'. It quickly became apparent to me that the 'tangible heritage', from ruined buildings to the celebrated Lindisfarne Gospels, were accompanied by something less obvious but equally interesting – the speech and culture of everyday working lives which still held the impression of past centuries.

In particular I was drawn to the traditional way of life of the local inshore fishermen, who worked from small open boats called 'cobles', and to their acute awareness that their heritage was under threat. These were mostly men in their 70s and 80s, whose knowledge, culture and language had been handed down for many generations. These men, more than the women, spoke a broad dialect, preserving words from 7th century Anglian Northumbria, as well as later traces of Old Norse and Dutch.

HS: how interesting that using dialect seems to some extent gendered! Is there anything more you want to say about this?

KP: Women's work was vital to traditional fishing communities. As well as running the house, it was the women's job to collect mussels from the shore and bait 1,400 hooks every day for the next morning's longlines while their men were at sea. This inescable, unpaid labour continued until the early 1950s. Many women spoke a less broad form of the dialect, perhaps because their social position was slightly more fluid than the men's.

HS: I thought of your work also when I visited Staithes, further down the coast, where the local museum provides fascinating insights into the lives of fishermen and their women; the often unacknowledged work of the women in the community struck me hard.

KP: I spent about ten years trying to record as much of the men and women's lives as I could, while supporting myself teaching night classes in the community. Half the poems in my first book, *The Lost Music,* and the long poem 'The Wund an' the Wetter' in *Two Countries,* were written during this period, and the fishing families' influence – particularly their respect for the sea and their pre-industrial regard for sustainability – remains with me, both in the poems in *Rhizodont* and in the prose which I'll share below.

HS: It's often striking (to me) how often dialectical variances surface in the names of everyday objects, such as birds, flora and fauna generally; can you explain this?

KP: Those words, learnt in childhood, are often the last to be lost, while the vocabulary of work disappears with the work itself.

HS: Of course – that makes sense! I Imagine the same is true in Cornwall and maybe parts of Wales where its industry has been lost! The survival of language is so related to the social and political situation of such communities?

KP: Some poems in *Rhizodont* draw on 'Pitmatic', the language of the North East coalfield. 'A Short Walk to the Sea's Edge', for instance, explores the losses of local speech and identity which accompany de-industrialisation and globalisation. This matters because language is central to a sense of community and identity. The Northumberland fishermen's language has all but disappeared in my lifetime, along with their way of life. Loss of community and displacement are part of the wider themes of evolution and extinction in *Rhizodont.*

HS: This is so significant. I was reading recently, in the magazine from the Tate Art Galleries, about the work of indigenous Australian artist, Emily Kam Kngwarray, whose first name (to which she would not respond) was her 'whitefeller' name, with Kam being her 'bush' name and Kngwarray her 'skin' name. It feels so important to honour the naming and the language of cultures displaced or crushed by colonialization and other forms of oppression and suppression.

KP: As a historian I've spent a large part of my life recording the vanishing traditions of this coast and working with communities to identify what the wider world can learn from them. At the same time, it's important not to romanticise the past. The loss of traditional inshore fishing, the most sustainable kind of fishing, happened as a result of industrialisation, which has been disastrous for fish stocks. But traditional fishing was dangerous for the men and brutally hard for the women. Coal mining ended for very different reasons, and is also frequently romanticised. Mining communities were close and supportive for a reason: mining was a dangerous, life-limiting job. Almost no one wanted their sons to follow them down the pit.

HS: That's an important reminder. I sense that as much as anything it is the soundworld, how the language feels in the mouth, that matters to you, given that much of your work has involved collaboration with composers: indeed, I believe your work has mostly arisen because of commissions. Tell us more about that.

KP: Yes, I loved the fishermen's language for its expressive musicality. You could understand what a fisherman like Charlie Douglas meant without knowing every word, because his dialect conveyed meaning through sound. For example, think of two coastal birds, the 'pickie' and the 'gormer'. One (the little tern) is light and deft, the other (the cormorant) dark and cumbersome. Can you feel the sense in the sound of those words? In its rhythm, too, the fishermen's speech was particularly expressive. 'The Wund an' the Wetter', with its strong anapestic metre, is made up of phrases which they used every day.

So you're right, I am drawn to the musicality of local language for sheer pleasure. I write for the ear more than for the page. Many of the sequences in *Rhizodont,* including all the second part of that book, were commissions, either for radio, live performance or podcast, often in collaboration with an audio artist. The sequence 'Susurrations of the Sea', which touches on the oceans' role in climate regulation, and which I've used to punctuate *Rhizodont,* began as a collaboration with radio producer Julian May. It can still be found on the BBC Sounds app. Between 2011 and 2021, I worked with an electronic composer, the late Peter Zinovieff, to create a series of multichannel poetry performances which I am currently adapting to make more publicly accessible. 'Under the Ice', the closing sequence in *Rhizodont*, was the last of these.

HS: I can confirm the BBC Sounds app still provides access to this – it is fascinating listening. I believe you are frustrated with the apparent schism between arts and sciences, which does neither any favours; it is clear in *Rhizodont* that you are working creatively from the knowledge you have, and passion for, the intersection between prehistory, science, and innovation, which is represented (if I have read this right) in the sections Ingenious and Under the Ice. I am struck by how seriously you take the research needed to inform this writing. How do you balance explaining that knowledge with creating art?

KP: When I was at school we had to choose between sciences and the arts at a young age. Because my maths was weak, I chose the arts; but I have always found that distinction between arts and sciences unhelpful. I've been lucky that in recent years I have been able to learn from scientists whose research has informed my poems. This came about through my collaboration with Zinovieff. Seeking a venue for our multichannel performances, I approached the planetarium in Life Science Centre, Newcastle, who generously agreed to host us. Through that connection I was able to work with Northumbria University's science outreach department, NUSTEM, to produce a series of pieces about the solar system and quantum physics. The idea was to translate scientific research to a non-science audience – and especially to encourage girls to study science. I learnt about each subject, not in order to write the poems, but through the process of writing them. The text of these pieces was published in my third Bloodaxe collection, *Edge.*

This work was very exciting to me. It allowed me to play with perspective and scale, from the unimaginably small (quantum particles) to the inconceivably large (universal forces of gravity and electromagnetism). I had long wanted to write a less anthropomorphic kind of poetry, and had been moving towards that in landscape-based sequences like 'Dunstanburgh' and 'Horse', which touch on deep, geological time. Zinovieff, who was originally a geologist, had influenced my thinking. I mentioned earlier that most of the poems in *Rhizodont* are deliberately not personal. With a few exceptions, since my first collection I have preferred not to write poems centred on a single personal 'I', but rather to use multiple perspectives and voices across much longer timescales. I want to create a poetry which can explore the planet and organic life without placing the human at its centre.

HS: As I indicated earlier, I think this absence of the dominant first person authorial voice is a really appealing aspect of your work; it makes space for all readers to find a footing, as it were.

KP: It is about trying to place the human in perspective, as part of something vastly greater than ourselves. The poems in the second part of *Rhizodont* form two sequences. The first, 'Ingenious', written for a podcast in association with the University of Salford, explores technologies of remote sensing, robotics and AI used in extreme environments such as contaminated nuclear sites and outer space. The second, 'Under the Ice', written with Northumbria University and NUSTEM, focuses on the use of some of those technologies to explore the landscape beneath the miles-deep ice of Antarctica, and so to understand more about Earth's climate.

Although these poems might appear very different from those in the first part of *Rhizodont*, just as those in *Edge* appear very different from *Two Countries*, I think of my science and landscape poems as a continuum. I find that living by the sea, next to Carboniferous rocks over 300 million years old, puts our own brief species into perspective. There have been at least three mass extinctions in the time since those rocks were formed, and we are currently experiencing another. Perhaps strangely, I find that immense perspective comforting.

HS: Yes, I resonate with that – do you know Julian of Norwich's image of the hazelnut in the palm of her hand as a symbol of all that exists? It's such a homely image and also something that reminds us of our own smallness and ephemerality, which has a positive as well as a negative side.

KP: That's a beautiful image. The evolution of life on Earth, and of our consciousness in particular, is such an extraordinary sequence of accidents, you could call it miraculous. I gave *Rhizodont* its title after the fossil fish which I mentioned earlier, which was discovered close to where I live. This huge, predatory creature belonged to a family called the Sarcopterygians, distinguished by fleshy fins, which eventually enabled them to make the transition from water onto land. All four-limbed creatures, including us, are descended from that family. This enormously important evolutionary shift strikes me as a metaphor for the technological transitions currently taking place in our lives – in our relations with our environment, in our movement away from fossil fuels, and perhaps particularly in the leap from embodied to artificial intelligence and agency, which has barely begun. Although the implications of this may be frightening, 'Ingenious' suggests the potential for positive feedback loops between human and machine intelligence and the planet's processes. For those who would like to discover more about the science, I provide notes, which are of course optional.

HS: You come across as someone who values the privacy of quiet spaces in which to be creative yet you have also attracted acclaim. How was it being shortlisted for the TS Eliot prize, an accolade most of us can only dream of? Do such public affirmations matter, or is the fact that you are making 'art' and sharing it more important?

KP: When *Rhizodont* was shortlisted for the T.S. Eliot prize I was genuinely astonished. Because I did not study English, because I've never held a University teaching post, because I don't publish much in poetry magazines, and perhaps because I live 50 miles from the nearest city, I've always felt somewhat outside 'the literary world' – whatever that is. Isn't feeling under the radar characteristic of most poets? It has always mattered more to me that my work should connect with the people around me, who might not otherwise read poetry. I love to publish my poems in local papers, bird-watching magazines, public spaces. When I first gave fisherman Charlie Douglas his poem, now in *The Lost Music*, he said very little; but he tucked it inside his cap and showed it to everyone who came to his hut. That mattered more to me than any subsequent accolade.

HS: That's a lovely image! I've often been more happy that a poem I wrote for a friend whose loved one had died went in the funeral service sheet because they found it helpful, than endless publications in journals that soon get put aside.

KP: Yes, that community function of poetry is an ancient one. It's interesting when a poem simultaneously serves a community and crosses a boundary to connect with a different audience. As we've discussed, the poems in *Rhizodont* are informed by many voices, whether those of former fishing and mining communities, or of research scientists. They were written to convey those voices to a wider audience, and assembled as a collection to connect them in unexpected ways. The T.S. Eliot prize shortlisting was a moment of acceptance from some very fine poets, and as such was a wonderful affirmation that those voices have indeed been heard outside their particular areas. Similarly, winning this year's Laurel Prize (for poetry about the environment) has given me confidence that the voices in my poems resonate across artificial boundaries of 'science' and 'arts', academic discipline or industrial jargon, geography, class or culture.

HS: Given how versatile you are in your output, I'm excited to learn that your next book will not be poetry; can you tell us more about it and the sections you have chosen to share with us here.

KP: I've wanted for many years to write a prose account of the local fishing community as I knew it. Prose allows for a more expansive exploration than poetry, and requires a different formal discipline. I'm basing my narrative, provisionally titled *The Black Huts,* on diaries, interviews and extensive note-taking from the time, which means organising an enormous amount of material. I work slowly, so it could be a long time before this book appears! I've chosen to share two extracts, both of which quote dialect speech. The first is an account of lobster fishing with 81-year-old Charlie Douglas and his brother Stephen aboard their coble, the *Jane Douglas,* and the second a story which touches on a particular female experience in the early 20th century.

HS: Katrina, thank you so much for sharing these pieces, which by a serendipitous event sit interestingly alongside Elaine Ewart's book, on the littoral community of Heligoland, which I have reviewed at the end of this issue. I have really enjoyed our conversation, which I am sure will provide food for thought for all our readers, whether poets or prose writers.

KP: Thank you, Hannah.

Saturday 25ᵗʰ August 1990
The harbour light snaps on suddenly in the dark, dazzling my eyes. It is 5.30 a.m. and the village is pitch-black and sleeping. This in-between hour feels very calm after a night of storm, in which I woke several times to streaks of lightning, bolting between sky and horizon. Now everything is completely silent, except for the constant low hush of the sea. As I cycle down to the harbour, rabbits scuttle out of my way. Hundreds of them. Who knew there were so many? Only they and the fishermen are awake at this hour.

Charlie sits quietly waiting for me on the pier, a squat, indistinguishable figure in knee-length oilskins which make him look like a priest. Stephen and their young crewmate Bally are already in the boat. The *Golden Gate* is nowhere in sight. I am late.

This is in any case a slow start for these men. Charlie has waited for a late tide to invite me aboard. I hurriedly tunnel inside the stiff yellow oilskin 'dopper', and clamber down the rusty ladder to the *Jane Douglas*. 'Gan forrard, ont' the deck,' orders Stephen. Beyond that, not a word is spoken.

I climb onto the precarious half-deck, wet on my knees, and balance between a stinking box of bait and the oars, mast and poy (boat hook), which are lashed down on the starboard side, pointing out to sea. Behind me lies a pile of old car tyres used for fenders, and on my right the fuel lead to the engine. The three men stand between thofts (seats) in the undecked stern half of the boat. Perched high in the bows, I feel vulnerable, precarious. The gunwale round the deck is only a few inches deep.

I barely have time to sit down before we leave the harbour. A raw cold envelops us as we head out to sea. The engine throbs beneath the deck, and a white plume of smoke billows backwards over the coble. The bow seems to rise up before us. Beyond the engine's noise and the bow wave, the sea is almost supernaturally calm. There is a magical stillness.

We head into a lightening patch of sky, a burning, azure blue, pierced, beyond the all-encompassing dark, by a single yellow star. The Morning Star. Not, in fact, a star at all, but the planet Venus. Behind us, the sea and land are one black expanse, but ahead the sea is silver, stippled, a restless net of light and shadow; and we drive into it, oars and mast fixed upon it. It feels as though we are streaming at top speed towards heaven.

Still nobody says a word. How calm the sea is. No spray touches me. The roll of the boat is soft, undulant, slewing through the water. Away off the port side, Longstone light flashes. Gradually, we draw ahead of it. The scattered orange lights of Beadnell and Seahouses are strung out in the distance in a single jewelled strand.

I stare back at them from this other world. Home. My sense that the village is changing, that something is vanishing, is a strong spur to try to record as much of the fishermen and women's lives as I can. I remember five or six cobles in the harbour from my childhood. Now there are only three and most of the men are old. Meanwhile the village has doubled in size, and many people, 'incomers' like me, settle here from elsewhere. I come to the fishermen wanting to understand these changes, sensing that they represent something more. It is something about our relationship to place and to nature that I want to explore.

All the time, the sky ahead of us is lightening, the sea's brilliance intensifying. Suddenly there in the distance ahead of us a black flag thrusts up out of the silver water.

'Gi' us a picket,' Stephen says.

He reaches for the dan (buoy) with the hooked stick and drags it and the luminous pink pellet aboard, laying them dripping on the deck beside me. The pellet is initialled CDB – Charlie Douglas, Beadnell. The dan is made out of cork and a black plastic sack, and rough, straight hazel sticks, still with the bark on them, lashed together with twine.

A heavy chain rattles noisily aboard. Stephen has vanished beneath the deck to put the engine into neutral. Its throbbing slows right down, and more white smoke and vapour rise from the exhaust, engulfing the whole port side of the boat, as if it were on fire. Charlie has stowed the tiller beneath the thoft; the hauler begins to turn, a rope strung around it, and there in the stern Charlie coils, rhythmically, monotonously, hand to hand. Off it comes for the strop, and the first pot is lifted. Bally heaves it, dripping, out of the water. In a single, effortless motion, Stephen unlaces it, removes the spent bait, throws it away, replaces it with a couple of whitings from the box, then unlaces the other half and pulls out a brick red crab. Then he fastens it again. It is beautiful to watch, that swift, spidery weaving motion of Stephen's fingers.

Crabs are like stones. They hang onto the mesh of the creeve (pot) with their claws and are sometimes very hard to break loose. At times, Bally has the next pot hauled and ready while Stephen is still wrestling with a crab that clings firmly to the creeve. He breaks it off by force, cracking its strong legs if need be. Sometimes, with a small one, there just isn't time, and he lets it go.

Lobsters, meanwhile, snap. The blue black creatures' claws are like scissors. They are angrier and quicker than crabs. They arch their backs and hump their tails, insect-like, waving their claws. Then they lie still, jerking occasionally in angry spasms.

The old men fish with six or seven fleets of 40 pots. Charlie has strong views on this. I think back to things he has told me in his tarry hut.

'It's nowt but greed,' he says. 'Now, at one time, when ye stopped the salmon fishin', then ye got the lobsterin' for maybe a month or two – till ye started the line fishin'. Used t' work 60 creeves. Some worked 50. Ye'd get plenty lobsters. An' now, some on 'em, 5 an' 600. Whae, it's only greed, woman. Aah've telled some on 'em that, an' aa'. The fishin's finished. An' fishermen's dyen it aa' theirsells. An' the lobsters – the boats that went t' the line fishin', th' was nivvor a lobster or a crab catched. But now, it's aa' yeer. The hyel yeer. Roond an' roond an' roond aboot. Now, in them days, October, November an' December, y' warn't allowed t' catch a crab. That was the closed season. That's when th' were stopped, y' see. But now, it's aa' yeer. An' fishermen's only got theirsells t' blame.'

He will tell anyone this.

'Y' bugger!' he'll shout, animated, as if suddenly remembering something important; 'W' used t' hoy aa' the berried hens away.'

The berried hens?

'The lobsters wi' the eggs on 'em. Look like little black berries ablow the tail. Whae, th' keep them now. Land the berried hens. Whae, if ye've got a hen sittin' on eggs, y' tyek the eggs, whae ye get naen chickens, wad ye? Whae it's the syem wi' them. Whae aye.' Charlie shakes his head. 'Whae it's best ye nivvor let on. Say nowt. Let them get on an' dae what th' like. It'll no worry me.'

It clearly does worry him, though. Now, as I watch him in the stern of the boat, silently coiling the tows as he has most mornings for the last 70 years, I'm moved by him in ways I can't fully explain.

The boat rocks gently as the creeves are hauled. Stephen stows them neatly on the port side, the first on the boards, the next two on top, with the outer one resting against the roller. There isn't much room to move as they come aboard, with coiled rope to one side and creeves to the other. The men work with an almost frantic haste, a machine-like smoothness. Gulls gather around the boat, greedy for the spent bait.

At six a.m. a tremendous dawn breaks over the water. The sun rises from a bank of lilac-coloured cloud, blood-red, spilling its trail on the sea. It turns the three men in their priestly yellow doppers to figures of bronze. There is a sudden warmth, a sense of benevolence. The men work on, oblivious to it. None of them, I notice, wears gloves. Stephen's wrists are bandaged with red flannel. He is hurling back green crabs, undersized lobsters, starfish, sea-urchins, a welter of small life. Sea spiders and similar unfamiliar, bristling creatures stalk out of the creeves on long legs, covering thofts and boards, the contents of a nightmare. Crabs roll on their backs, their claws and legs flailing – they, too, are spider-like, prehistoric. Their eyes bulge, impotent. In the stern, the hauler spins, slowly dripping, and Charlie winds the rope with a small, tight, repetitive movement of his hands, broken only by the rhythmic jerk as the strop of the next pot is lifted clear.

Tuesday 26th October 1993

'Five lobsters the day! Five! Aah telled ee what ye'd git, this time a th'eer, sea flat like that!'

Stephen rubs the creeve he is mending with a stiff brush, dusting off the dry tufts of brown ware that fringe it. The heat in Charlie's hut hits you like a wall when you open the door. It makes you feel drunk and giddy. The stove's braided blue smoke rasps at your throat. Stephen is ensconced in his niche next to it. How he can withstand its heat I do not know. Charlie squats on his seat on its other side. Tom, Douggie and Benty Jack are lined up on chairs, Barty, Bill and I propped up on the sawdust benches. They are talking about characters they remember from their youth.

'Roadsters, w' used t' caal 'em,' says Tom. 'Tramps, y' kna. Th' was one little fella, canny little fella, Aah used t' fetch him a mug a coffee an' a sandwich. He used t' alwess hev a barra, a little wooden barra. Danny Carlin, th' caa'd im.'

'Danny was the only man allowed t' come t' Beadlin,' says Charlie. 'He come alang t' the huts there: 'O aye, wheer y' sleep Danny?' 'The Cave at Seahooses.' 'O it wad be rough?' 'No, it was aa'right, man.' Whae, it was wheer the rubbish was aal tipped in, them days, an' th' was hundreds a bloody caldies (rats) in there! Put a bit tin ower the top 'n his heed. Hard, eh? Whae, folk wad nivvor believe how hard th' wore, y' kna.'

Barty is busy sawing 'wadges' to hammer into the hazel bows where they are fixed into the creeve bottoms. He carves them carefully along the grain of the wood. Cut them any other way and they are no good: they will snap as you hammer them home. Stephen sharpens each one with his knife and fills his pockets: 'Ye want a good point on 'em.' Then he sits with a creeve between his knees, doubling the twine along the top rail. He measures the twine along the length of the creeve: two lengths, then he cuts it with his knife, and seals the end against the hot stove. When he has knit each length in, he cuts off the end with the glowing tip of a wire which rests on the ashes in the orange grate.

Day after day of leaden skies, hardly any wind, just a wisp from the north, northeast or northwest. The sea is flat. The glass is very high – 30.9 – but it is cold out there.

'The farther the ring fro' the moon,' Benty says, 'the nearer the storm.' This raw, high-pressure weather, he tells me, is what the old men used to call 'a Northeast Piner.'

Behind him the stove smokes, orange-red and fierce. The men went down at three this morning, then lay for hours until it got light and didn't get back in from hauling creeves until after 11.

'D' ye kna what a heck is?' Tom asks me. 'A manger on the waa' for t' feed the cattle. For the stray, y' kna (straw). Th' was four tramps lyin' i' the heck one time – farmer come, gettin' the hay oot wi' the hay-fork. Stuck his boot sole straight through. Tramp i' the stray, properly happed up. Be aa' the syem if it was his gut.'

Images flash through my mind: the lost and homeless, an anonymous city, Newcastle or London, perhaps; street children picking over rubbish tips in distant countries . Not here, in rural England. But here, too, within living memory, the dispossessed shunned the district workhouse, to sleep on a rubbish dump in a cave, or in a manger.

'Th' was a woman an' aa',' says Charlie. 'Deef as a post, she was, used t' gan aboot sellin' bits a things – pins an' needles an' things.'

'O aye!' says Tom. 'Nelly the Sweep! Pushed hor stuff aroond in a pram. She was weel-liked. An' she had a dowter.'

A daughter! Charlie tells her story with an intensity that is almost Biblical.

'Theer's a hemmel (barn) away yon side a Christon Bank', he begins. 'Sooth side. Ye kna at one time there used t' be a lot a roadsters gaa'n aboot. Ony amoont. An' there used t' come aroond heor, Aah divvin't kna hor right name, but Nelly the Sweep, she gat. One time in the winter time when the snaa was on the groond, in thon hemmel, i' the field, at Christon Bank: auld Norman Henderson showed us that hemmel. An' th' was a lot a snaa on the groond. An' the herrod (shepherd) come through wi' the dog, lookin' at his flocks. An' he started t' bark, the dog, an' the aa'd herrod thought th' might be a badger or somethin' in the hemmel. An' when he went – auld Nelly the Sweep – Nelly the Sweep – she just had had a bairn.'

He pauses. The shock of it, all these years later.

'An' he walked back t' Christon Bank, the herrod, an' he phoned for a doctor an' polis an' one thing an' another. An' when he come back she was gone. Wi' the bairn, mind. Saw the footprints i' the snaa'. Them was hard folk, eh?'

Nelly the Sweep, deaf as a post, selling pins and needles and things. Pushing her meagre belongings around in a pram.

'She was weel-liked. An' she had a dowter.'

A daughter, born in the snow, in the memory of these men. A life now almost lost to memory, begun a hundred years ago, in a hemmel that still stands, yon side of Christon Bank.

Katrina Porteous

Holy War
(The LF Club, Kharkiv, Ukraine, September 2023)

'Foreign' is understood. They're just *the Legion*, resting their weary Kalashnikovs against the bar. Ben high-fives Ricardo over an empty chair. Guy's wrist has healed OK so they crack a beer, walk through last Tuesday's knife fight in the trenches. Freya disses the dumplings and predicts the fall of Kupiansk, again, while the bug-eyed medic informs his vodka: *Everyone who comes to Ukraine has a hole in their soul.*

Get a round in. A local on the swing bench calls Grandma to check she's alive. Another pastes Putin's mug on the dartboard. Ricardo fucks off for a piss and Ben scratches – metal plate in his skull keeps itching, and the dick in the lower bunk screamed all night. Lost half his unit in the last offensive. Scroll the chat… wounded Czech selling off armour… residence permits… arsehole with PTSD calling everyone war tourists. Fuck this, just chill for an evening. Love this place, though it's too well known, there'll be a missile through the roof one of these nights. The medic's getting friendly with Freya. That joker Mitch sticks on 'Hotel California'.

Two tours of Afghanistan were enough. Then the TV showed kids trudging through rubble

and Ben thought No and got off the sofa and somehow kept rising... Maybe he'll sign a three-year contract with Kraken. Maybe Freya will shut up about Kupiansk. Ric appears with beers. Ben yells at the medic, *Who the fuck's gonna stand up to Putin if we don't?*

Hell yeah!s all round. Mitch cranks up the volume on 'Hotel California'. Ben weeps for his divorce in Leeds. After they cleared out those katsaps* from Izium, a few local kids came home. This little girl hugged him.

Anna Bowles

* *A derogatory term for Russians.*

Last Meeting

SPECIAL NEEDS
(Zaporizhzhia, Ukraine, September 2024)

The teachers' diffident torch-beam
skids from the fractured pipework
to the stub of the classroom door.

They salvage an aluminium table,
gape through the window frame
at a ring binder lodged in a tree.

The keyboards have melted to dung.
The hit was Saturday, so the colleagues
burned alive weren't teaching online.

One blackboard's not entirely charred.
As they left on invasion day, the children
chalked lopsided hearts.

Anna Bowles

FIRST-AID TRAINING FOR TEACHERS
(Dnipro, Ukraine, April 2025)

Go on, poke the wound.
A 3D-printed silicon cube
gouged like a rose. Seek

the nestling nub of artery.
Pinch hard: it'll be gouting.
Pack in gauze with your free hand.

Get a colleague to hold
the child down… If you can't?
Picture the triage doctor

in your school's shot-up cafeteria
slowly shaking her head.
Do you have any questions?

Anna Bowles

Two Years, Ten Months, Fifteen Days of Sorrow
(January 2025)

The fabulous smell of a mint salad and butter cake from the kitchen
but I never thought that a direct flight home would become my un-reality
It is freezing today in Oxfordshire and the crust of frost is on the roofs
it must be freezing outside the Siberian cell and it might be the same frost
I drink my milk oolong and watch Kaos and The Penguin
but I have a balloon with salty water inside my chest and it's hard to breathe
It is a library day and I go to Duke Humphrey's to see some incunabula
It has been two years since my classmate burned her Russian passport
At the weekend, we will listen to Einaudi in the Royal Concert Hall
A pianist has also recently died in a Siberian cell because he did not agree
After, we will meet with our friends who are going to stage my book
and in my country you can get five years of prison for a theatre play
At Sainsbury's, I buy brown oranges and Chapel Down
and my mother can't afford to buy milk and butter
When I go to have my hair cut red pixie as usual
and I put the ashes of burned Ukrainian cities on my head
I will make new make-up in a French style for the evening
and I have a veil heavy like an iron curtain on my face
In the dark, I will sleep peacefully dreaming about the end of this
and I don't know what my little niece is dreaming about

Soe Frost

LEBANESE CAFÉ, LONDON

I'm sipping fresh-snipped mint tea
sweetened with rosewater and sugar
from a silver pot embossed with jasmine stars.
Its elegant spout arches a flamingo's neck.

Yoghurt arrives with a green sprinkle
of pistachios, and floats on date syrup.
Pomegranate tiles, a scent of caraway and anise
make-believe this London café is in Byblos.

I look up and see the profile of a man
with a handsome face, his black beard
corkscrew-curled and sharply trimmed.
As he strides by, I recognise him –

an Assyrian lion-hunter
from the frieze in the British Museum.

Sue Norton

AGE OF
EMPIRE
*(In 1772-3
Robert Clive
faced
parliamentary
scrutiny over
the
acquisition of
his vast
wealth)*

Anyone would think I'd draped myself
with the jewels of Jaipur

to listen to these detractions
from such august gentlemen,

or furnished one's modest salons
with plunder from a Bengal palace.

Good Sirs, do you imagine my chamber pots
are fashioned with sapphires and gold?

I flatter myself to have written
rules for princes, but I am no king.

Is it not a source of pride
to take surrender of an army?

Did I not deliver a continent
to grace His Majesty's domains?

A city's riches lay spread
as a harvest feast before me,

merchants and ministers
played for my smiles.

I was shown through the galleries
of a state's ancient treasury,

vaults flowing with gems
and artefacts from the start of time.

The Nawab himself invited me
to present an inventory of wishes.

Certainly, I could have doubled
my fortune in the hour it took

to walk those halls.
If truth be told, Mr Chairman,

I stand astonished
at my own moderation.

Victor Tapner

VESPA VELUNTINA
(Asian Hornet)

you can't hide behind
musical syllables

I know who you are

the great invader
from the Himalayas
the illegal immigrant
arriving in a French port
with a shipment of ceramics
a storm in a teacup

I'm watching you right now
circling the hive
no night-time assassin
but flaunting yourself
in broad daylight
all Shakespearean with your
chest of black velvet and
legs dressed in yellow hose

you think you've found
a soft target
but I'm watching you

Catherine Glavina

1. First Meeting: Sea World County Hall

Bulbs of slit eyes, tentacles curled
round head, abject and despondent
he hovers over minimal
rocks, mimicking sleep while watching
the boredom of a metre-cubed
tank. His colour matches the rock,
sometimes he is orange ochre.
What hope of communication?

2. Miracles of Intelligence

Octopuses have eight brains, one
in each tentacle; overall
coordination by a ninth.
A union of sovereign states,
flexible freedom, unity
of purpose. So much thought, a
think tank and a neural network
invented long before AI.

3. Sea World Aquarium Plymouth

She likes some keepers, squidging up
to them; with others she hides in
a corner of the tank, taking
food grudgingly, with an eye out
for escape. Having no bones she
can squeeze through tiny holes, but tubes
(provided for amusement of
the punters), she treats with disdain.

4. Mathematical Theories

Octopuses use the octal
number system, rather than the
decimal, counting tentacles
rather than fingers. Plato told:
only five regular solids
are possible in 3-D space;
of these the octahedron has
eight equal triangle faces.

5. *On the Perfect Nature of Eight*

Noble gases, like krypton and
neon, have eight electrons in
their outer shell, and will never
react. The octopus too is
solitary, but humans have
only four tentacles – so we
need another to be complete,
making the beast with eight limbs.

6.*We Very Rarely Eat Our Spouse*

We very rarely eat our spouse,
but octopus love ends in a
meal. Sad for both, mating triggers
accelerated senescence
from youth and beauty to death in
a few months. Love an octopus
wisely. If they like you, they like
touch – sociable and curious.

7. *Dietary Consequences*

I decide never again to
eat octopus - add to the list
of things I'll just not touch: foie gras,
battery eggs, crated veal and
intensively reared chicken. Yet
I still find roast lamb succulent.
All morality has to lead
to hypocrisy in some way.

8. *Engaging with the Modern World*

On *YouTube* an octopus eats
a small shark. Today's Guardian
shows them using all manner of
junk on the sea bed to make homes.
Under my duvet I writhe, legs,
arms, independent slithering
trying to think, feel, octopus –
de-colonise the octopus.

Keith Willson

They came in *waka* made from the land
With hands deft, skilled and strong
Through winds and fearsome waves
They came, forced back and then returned
They followed the paths of the stars
Saw clouds thicken, thin, rise, fall
Watched birds swoop down to rest
Saw signs of life in the ocean
Heard songs of whales and dolphins
Felt the swell of the sea in their sex
A cluster of clouds and they were close.

Finally, a thin white cloud of an island
Aotearoa, the new land
The trill of the *tui*, the call of the *kea*
Rang out from the calm of the shrub
Forests dense and green reached towards
The never-ending sky of bluest blue.

They had arrived.

Tina MacNaughton

(Aotearoa; land of the long white cloud, the Maori word for New Zealand).

IT'S RAINING

it's raining tears of the gods
        at the mess we are making

it's raining tears of the angels
        at the loss of compassion

it's raining tears that are sullied
        with chemicals, microplastics, particulates

it's raining tears in downpours
        flooding out of control

it rains no tears at time of drought
        it's all cried out

Terry Sherwood

Time is a tough negotiator, poker-faced with its locks and binding contracts. It knows all the tricks, sitting with its back to the rising Sun and speaking in a low voice that necessitates leaning into the zone of intimidating discomfort. It drums its nails on its desktop, sharp reports like a distant firing squad starting early to fulfil unreasonable quotas, then it rocks back ever-so-slightly in its chair and fixes its eyes on a point between the late Cretaceous and the date pencilled in for my demise. *We need*, it says, in a voice like a dreaming wolf, *to review the situation*, only it breaks that final word into four distinct syllables, each one standing like a siltstone block on a windswept plain. There's a figure in the distance, but they're too far away to assess as friend or foe and, besides, my eyes are sand-whipped and streaming. The sky is a wounded snake, coiling to strike. *Sign here*, says Time in a voice that brooks no negotiation, and we're back in the room. Their right hand holds a dying sunflower, their left a souvenir biro from a resort that was popular in the 60s. Somewhere, there's a stutter of gunfire.

Oz Hardwick

CHECKPOINT FEAR

After Bataclan
        a sombre advent at Brandenburg Gate.
No carol singers. No candlelit menorah.
                We turn to
the French embassy where
        there are flowers, votive candles;
a sympathy tricolour at the Russian embassy
        and a quote from Verlaine: *je pleure.*
                We turn
towards Friedrichstrasse:
        no young people *en carnaval,*
past vitreous consumerism,
                and turn
into Gendarmenmarkt at Christmas,
        a man is selling the German Big Issue,
        another man asks for a mite of money.
                We turn
to mulled wine therapy
        in the marble light of Schiller's statue.
At Checkpoint Charlie I pose in a Rommel cap
        smile at the insincere deference
        of two fake soldiers,
                then turn
into a brand-new Black Box exhibit,
        decked out in Soviet red and Yankee blue,
exhibiting dossiers of the Cold War.
                So we turn and turn
shoulder to shoulder as if in an infinity mirror
        and here there are black boxes
                of the future of Checkpoint
                                Fear.

Michael Henry

Begun in London – all done
one morning hour: beaten, spat on,
dragged to the scaffold, ale-jeered
through the rope's teasing mercy,
the blade's gutting liberation
lightening the procreational load.

Still alive to see the entrails burning,
before the Almighty takes heart
into the executioner's hands, dividing
the rest to boil and salt for the gallop
against rotting time to those native parts
they tried so hard to free.

Spiked between rows of gating stone:
crow-torn, fly-blown, each putrid
wind-shorn quarter blackens and dries.
Pride of place, the empty sockets
stare down each gawping face below.

Frost-scalped, the final scraps
of recognition fall past withered lips
risking – who knows? – one last rictus grin
before the dropped jaw's forgotten
gape at the right, the wrong, horizon.

Craig Dobson

BAGGAGE

I've tried to put some order to the vast
and tangled mess that forms our history,
to catalogue our long and complex past
with prejudice but not dishonesty,
to carefully preserve the touching hands,
the parted lips, the kindest of the words,
to archive in a way that understands
why anger doesn't need to be reheard.
I won't let moths turn linen into rags
or store our Sunday best with dirty socks.
I'll loosely pack the love in open bags
and cram the hate in chests with heavy locks
then hold the love while equally disposed
to keep the chests of hate forever closed.

Chris Scriven

On the evening of the Sixth Day, God was pleased with His work, especially humans, which had been pretty complicated to make. But at supper, during the milk and honey course, his trainee came in looking worried, and told him he'd forgotten to make bees. It's a risk telling an Infallible that they've forgotten something and she was resigned to the inevitable thunderbolt but Lo! in his Infinite Wisdom God was not angry. Yea, He said, I'll do it after we've eaten. She accepted His answer, having no alternative, but was sceptical that He would remember, the rate He was turning water into wine. But she'd only had experience of two previous creations, whereas His was Manifold so who was she to question? Later, when she heard snoring from the Deity Quarters, she took a risk and decided to have a go at making bees herself. She hadn't qualified in the necessary Advanced Creative Skills yet but she had access to Spare Parts on the Seventh Level and that day she'd been helping in a show and tell workshop for Saints' children. She riffled through some paintings from it and picked one by St Anne's daughter - clearly a yellowy insect of some sort - and went upstairs to see if she could piece something together. She worked all night and ended up with wasp wings and legs, eyes from dragonflies, and a felty kind of yellow stripy body which she copied from the Experimental Caterpillar folder. The result was ungainly, like a knitted rail freight wagon with wings, but it did actually fly if stoked up with enough sugar. Next morning, which was, after all, the Seventh Day when He was supposed to be Resting, she asked Him about his Bee Creation at breakfast. There was a silence while the whole refectory held its breath and then He said He thought she was having a go at it. She knew it was a misuse of Omniscience but didn't say anything and produced her bee when He asked to have look at it. And Lo! He laughed instead of thunderbolts, and it was Good, and the refectory breathed again. Later, He had Gabriel appear to thank her and add that it probably would work long enough for this particular iteration of Creation because on reflection He thought He hadn't quite got humans right yet.

William Coniston

It's breezy on Portobello beach. Inland,
    cherry blossoms sway.
Prickly spires bruise the sky purple:
    the ischemic underbleed of sunset.
The mild din of the town behind, the
    uncouth slurping of the sea.
On the mossy pier a cormorant embraces
    the coming night.

But for a pregnant cloud lumbering to some
    rain-minded conspiracy, that boy
skimming the frothing edge, a drunken tramp
    demanding from the crimson horizon
a glimpse of destiny, his border collie
    corralling an anxious tide of memory,
and my heart, rapid after your text breaking
    with me, it would be perfect.

Agana Agana

neither of us felt like cooking so we walked into
town although it was tricky avoiding all our
anniversaries and birthdays so we chose the pub
by the river where we'd never eaten before just
sat outside with a pint on summer evenings
watching the geese go honking home in a line
you were talking to the waitress while I was
trying to move my face she showed us to a table
away from the window we sat at right angles
facing into the room dreading seeing anyone we
knew like having an affair but less exciting I
ordered a starter Chinese spring rolls with chilli
sauce and didn't eat it perhaps there was wine I
was waiting for the day to be over we'd already
made up separate beds I guess I shouldn't linger

Elaine Ewart

My friends have been instructed
when they meet you at a party, to let fall
some key facts. The mansion on the hill
I bought for a song. My flame-haired girlfriend
who owns Ikea. The heart-stopping rum punch
at my literary salons. I'm on the cover of Time,
Vogue and Farming Today. The council raised
my statue in gold in the market square.
My breakup poem with oystercatchers
has won the Forward Prize. A gif
of my Oscar acceptance speech
has been memed. A newly discovered
ichthyosaur is named after me.
I am blonder and younger.

No-one here has heard of you
and if they had, they wouldn't be interested.

Elaine Ewart

The floorboards sold it to me, stripped
throughout the house, slates unhooked
for a skylight, spilling sun down the stairs

into Victorian dark, a corsetted drawing room
where a woman once gossiped with afternoon friends —
doilies and porcelain teacups, napkins on nested tables,
a personal blend of tea.

That's where it all began, the curtains drawn in the bay,
an end of the evening affair, hard to believe the marks
she made, under my mane of hair. I blame it on the dress
we bought that afternoon, eighties slippery stuff,
second-hand silver and black, its squeeze across my thighs

and the neck, oh the neck that slumped
a long way down my back.

Jenny Hockey

His splash was much smaller than David's

The floors in my house won't stop moving –
they're wild ocean waves that flip me over
and down I go, breaking more bones.

The towel that muted the snap is used
to dry my feet knowing I can't stand,
or swim any further

and there's a seagull enjoying my splinters,
whilst the warm air shamelessly drifts in
holding a *DANGER: DEEP WATER* flag.

On the sandy floor
my strong hands dig a tunnel out
with a swell of *useless* building behind.

I try to reach a hard rock
to heave this wreck of a body up;
my wet eyes now covered in missing you.

The *NO EXIT* sign throbs, as I envy
the view from my seat and know a leg
wrapped tight will never leave.

These bones held together will have to wait
as outside becomes a dangerous sight.
Fragments of coffee shops litter my floor.

Julie Stevens

MOTHER'S DAY

See-saw, a sleepless night,
Jenny has got a new master,
breakfast fraught, spooning goo,
but she can't work any faster.

To market, to market, the cupboard is bare
the butcher, the baker, the grocer;
shopping with baby takes three times as long,
just get the whole thing over.

Home again, home again, naps when he shouldn't,
she hopes he sleeps a bit longer,
makes the most of it, getting jobs done,
knows she'll pay for it later

Upstairs, downstairs, in and out,
loading, wiping, folding,
washer, hoover, cooker, iron;
he wakes refreshed, she's flagging.

Clap the hands, playtime again,
the same games every day
monotony addles her brain;
she's Sleepy, Grumpy, Dopey.

Pat-a-cake pat-a-cake dinner time,
he'll eat no fat or lean,
spreads his food around the room,
leaves his platter clean.

Watching the clock till daddy comes home
Bo Peep has lost the plot,
the wheels on the bus are coming off,
hickory dickory dock.

Nursery rhymes, storytime,
how many miles to bed?
Hush a bye baby, one last push,
to get to The Land of Nod.

Bathtime, bathtime, rub-a-dub-dub,
lavender oil and bubbles,
wind him down or wear him out,
she can't decide, too fuddled.

Wee Willie Winkie, in bed by eight
oh, what a good boy is he;
Sleeping Beauty can't wait to lie down,
she knows she'll be up by three.

Ann Gibson

The three-year-old
circled the house that
grew fat on summer soil
and shadows, trailing
his fingers over ruptured
crystals and blue bumps
on the walls, rolling the
word "stucco" around
on his tongue, relishing
its percussive bursts
deep in his throat,
knowing that he was
on the verge of some
metamorphosis meant
for him alone.

Kyle Heger

When I was five, Mum left me too long in the car:
something troubling, grown-up like *money…accounts…*
The back of the passenger seat was a grid:
tiny diamonds over grey-blue abyss.
I stared so hard, willing some wallpaper
rhino to charge. But I slipped through the mesh.
Its gauzy veil upon my face, I was trapped in the well.

So when you talk for hours – your *mortgage…*your *ex* -
and I nod like a novelty dog on the dash,
know at least from where I listen. All I really strain to hear
is the brisk clop of heels and the car door's release.

Fionnuala Kearney

I have lived life as a tree,
my charms carved in wood.
My father was a god,
you see. Poor me.
Not much fun being famous,
always in the spotlight,
mere mortals muttering
'Where's good time Daphne?'

I was a follower of Artemis.
Hunting was my passion.
That's how I got my thrills.
No time for matrimony,
until an arrow shot from Cupid's bow
turned my world topsy-turvy.
Suddenly, I was the prey,
the son of Zeus after me.

In vain, I shouted out to Peneus,
'Dad, I'm in a bit of bother.'
Why did I waste my breath?
He took no notice of me
and Apollo kept on coming,
like the Terminator, he'd never stop.
You might think the river god
would have risen from the deep to save me.

Not so. There on a mossy bank,
Apollo was upon me.
My lips were icicles. His smouldered.
One spark inflamed a burning kiss.
A millisecond of ecstasy was all it took
and we were of sound mind again,
exclaiming 'Well, that was freaky.'
Then, Apollo said `Great vibes,'

while I suggested 'Yeah, let's hang out'.
My last words. I was struck dumb,
arms becoming branches,
breasts made of bark, hair wisped
into green laurel leaves.
Apollo plucked a sprig
and stuck it in his golden curls.
'Too bad' he said, 'She was a total babe.'

Miriam Sulhunt

When I got off the tube at Belsize Park, my right arm stayed on the train. From the platform, I could see it, the hand clutching the yellow rail inside the carriage.

"Hey, get out of there," I shouted. "Get out of the train, it's our stop."

The doors slid shut. Through the window, I saw the hand detach itself from the rail and give a sheepish wave. The train began to move and I ran alongside it for a few metres still shouting, but I was handicapped by having to carry all my bags in one hand.

I went to the station office to report the missing limb.

"Arm," said the man behind the window. "Are you aware that the carrying of weapons on the underground is illegal. There is a penalty. I forget how much but I could look it up for you."

"Not that sort of arm. This – " I pointed with my left hand to the torn right armhole of my pale blue shirt. I did not invite him to look inside it because I did not want to look inside myself.

"I got on the train at Hendon. Northern line, Morden via Bank, the one that's just been through here."

"You'd better give me your name," he said. Suddenly he seemed in rather a hurry, "And contact numbers. When we have … um … apprehended the er … , that is to say, if we find your uh ... property, we will let you know."

There was nothing more to do, so I went home. I make that sound easy; it wasn't. When you are accustomed to having a right hand, simple tasks without it become very complicated. I'd already had difficulty getting through the exit barrier, having to manipulate my pass, together with my briefcase and two plastic bags full of shopping. Out in the road I found myself unbalanced by the weight of this baggage and walking with a leftward lurch, as though I was drunk.

The worst moments came when I strove to get into my house. Normally I turn the yale key with my right hand while simultaneously pressing down the door handle with my left. Now I tried to move swiftly from yale to handle or handle to yale, in an effort to get both latches back at the same time. Either way I was just not quick enough and was reduced to holding down the handle with my chin, while manipulating the yale key with my one hand. A passer-by who did not know me might well have concluded I was breaking and entering. Fortunately, there was nobody around.

I will not go into detail about how I struggled to empty the shopping bags, using my teeth to aid my hand. Afterwards, feeling exhausted and cross, I took a glass and a bottle of wine into the den and by dint of clutching the bottle between my knees, I managed to unscrew the cap.

As I was downing the second glass, there came a series of soft thumps on the front door. When I opened it, there was an arm, floating at about knee height above the front doorstep. It was clad in red satin.

The expression "to know something like the back of your hand" is very misleading. I did not immediately recognise the hand which protruded from the shiny sleeve. It was only the unique intaglio ring on its fourth finger that convinced me it was mine.

"Don't expect me to be glad to see you. I've been made to look like a lunatic and a burglar, even a potential terrorist, because of you."

The arm glided up to shoulder height and hovered there uncertainly.

'Never do that again," I said.

The hand raised itself in a peace gesture. Then with a squelch and a click, the arm reattached itself to my shoulder.

Later, as we were finishing the bottle of wine, my Significant Other asked, "Why are your arms wearing odd sleeves?"

"Well," I began, "to cut a long story short …"

Paula Morris

It was tonight, when I came in through the back door from the garden, that I thought I glimpsed, out of the corner of my eye, something small slipping in at the same time. I thought it was one of the neighbour's cats. He never lets them in the house. They roam all over the show and use my flower beds as a toilet.

I looked around a bit. I couldn't bring myself to say, "Here, kitty, kitty," even though I was thinking it. I couldn't see anything so I returned and locked the door. I had only taken three or four steps back into the kitchen when I felt a sharp pain in my right shin.

I looked down just in time to see a black shape, a shadow almost, disappear from view. My shin was aching badly. When I rolled my trouser leg up to take a look, I saw it was bleeding from a fresh wound. I'm not very good with blood. Especially my own. Especially when it's on the outside. I started to feel a bit woozy.

I hobbled through to the dining room and sat down smartly on a chair by the table. It was then I felt another sharp pain. This time in my left shin. Again, I just caught sight of a black shadow before it disappeared. Same story: I rolled up my left trouser leg, my left shin was now bleeding.

What the hell was going on? I didn't know what to do. Clean and dress the wounds seemed the obvious first thing. Then worry about their cause.

I had just stood up, very shakily, both legs hurting, feeling woozier and woozier, when it happened again.

It was the back of my right leg this time, the calf. The pain was excruciating. I sat back down immediately. The pain, the shock, and the loss of blood, were all combining to make the room begin to darken and turn. I could see the teeth marks in my calf. I put my head between my knees to prevent myself from fainting, while trying to keep guard on my legs in case of another attack.

It must have climbed the chair, for the next stabbing pain came at the top of my left buttock, just below the hip. I felt the place with my hand. I couldn't sit up to see but I could feel the blood. I made the mistake of looking at my hand. The sight of all the blood was too much for me. I slid off the chair onto the floor. The room was getting darker all the time. The floor felt like the deck of a ship at sea, it wouldn't stay still. I stretched my arms out, palms flat against the parquet flooring, to try and steady myself.

There was a sudden pain in my right shoulder. A black shadow again. No sooner glimpsed than gone. What kind of creature behaved like this? Why was it attacking me? What did it want? I was having more and more trouble thinking. My pulse was racing, I was sweating, my skin felt clammy.

Then I felt something new. It was my shins at first. The left one and then the right. A licking sensation. Something was licking the wounds. It felt soothing. It immediately helped with the pain. I couldn't see anything due to the position I was lying in and the oppressive greyness of the light.

But then it started licking the wound on my shoulder. I turned my head so I could see. I had difficulty focusing but I managed more or less. The creature looked a bit like a black cat. The fur was sticking out, giving it a prickly look, rather like a cartoon cat that had had an electric shock. The most extraordinary thing was its face. It stopped licking for a moment and looked at me. It was smiling. Or rather, it had a wide, fixed grin on its face that revealed a row of sharp, pointy teeth, covered in my blood. There was also blood on the fur all around its mouth, which gave it the ridiculous appearance of wearing lipstick, emphasising the grin, a grin that reminded me of Tenniel's illustration of the Cheshire Cat. It had black eyes that were hard to see in the black fur. I could just see a soft glint where they were.

It suddenly disappeared from my view and I felt it licking the wound on my left buttock. Again, it felt soothing. Very soothing. I began to relax. I began to feel sleepy. I stopped worrying and drifted peacefully off to sleep.

I'm awake again now. I'm here, although I'm not sure where here is. I can't move but I don't seem to mind. It's warm and sunny. I think I'm in the garden.

It must be the garden, because there's the washing line stretching down alongside the path. A woman appears from behind me carrying a white laundry basket. She begins pegging out the washing. She works her way methodically down the line. I see her in profile as she hangs out each article. I'm so pleased to see her that I begin to weep, although I can't think who she is.

She's doing a beautiful job, you can see she knows what she's doing. Each garment, sheet, towel, is neatly pegged out, fully exposed to the sun so it will dry with the minimum of creases. As she hangs it up, the washing seems to be attracting butterflies. A cabbage white has landed on a sheet. It's sunning itself, gently opening and closing its wings. A common blue alights on a blue towel. A brimstone settles on a yellow T-shirt that has just been pegged out. I wonder, idly, where the peacock I can see fluttering above the line is going to land. A bit of a challenge, that.

"Bloody butterflies," I hear myself say, "They get everywhere." It's definitely me, it's definitely I who spoke, but I don't recognise the voice.

The woman laughs and continues her task of hanging the washing out to dry. She looks so beautiful in the sunshine. It shines through her hair creating a halo effect. She is wearing a white blouse and a pleated cotton skirt embroidered with flowers. Her hands are nimble and efficient, moving skilfully. I notice she's wearing a blue diamond on the ring finger of her left hand.

She doesn't stop until she reaches the end of the line. She turns then and starts walking back up the path towards me, the empty basket under one arm. I still don't know who she is, but she is making me feel incredibly happy. She smiles at me as she approaches. She's waving.

Don Rodgers

The Book Vault stood a few blocks off MacDougal Street in the heart of Greenwich Village. A stone stairway descended from the sidewalk to the shop, which was located in the basement of an old, converted brownstone. The Vault sold used books with esoteric themes and had a large selection of local titles with names like "Haunted Mansions of Manhattan." Its primary customers were neighborhood bohemians and students from NYU.

Marcus looked up from his inventory when he heard the tinkle of the bell over the door. An old man entered. There was a haunted look in his eyes. He had a shaggy white beard and stringy hair and wore a weathered overcoat that seemed custom designed for shoplifting. Marcus knew the few books of any value were kept locked in a glass case, but he decided to keep an eye on the man nevertheless.

The old man perused the walls of books. He squinted narrowly at the spines as though near-sighted and worked his way down the shelves until he had examined every title. He then began rummaging through the books piled on a bargain table in the center of the store.

A couple of women came into the shop and Marcus had to deal with their questions and purchases. He lost track of the old man. As the second woman carried her bag from the establishment, Marcus noticed the man standing, watching him.

"I'd like to see the rare books," he croaked in a voice gnarled by cigarettes and foul weather. "The ones in the case."

"Is there a particular title you're interested in?"

"Just let me see the books."

Marcus unlocked the glass. The man lifted the volumes, one by one, reading the spines. Marcus wondered if he intended to snatch a book and make a dash for the door. The idea of wrestling with the greasy old derelict was an unpleasant prospect.

The man examined the final tome and set it down. Marcus closed and locked the case.

"Perhaps you could tell me specifically what you're looking for."

In a tone of hopeless despair, the old man named a title.

"I've never heard of it," said Marcus.

"It was published in 1967," said the man. "It went out of print five years later, you bastards."

It was a bizarre choice of word. Marcus became acutely aware of the physical fact of being alone with the man. More to distract him than anything else, he said, "Let me run a search through my database and see what I can find."

He pulled up the search engine on his computer, all the while keeping his eyes on the strange customer. He discovered the book had indeed been published in 1967 and was out of print. He ran a search to see if he could find it for sale anywhere in the country. It turned up nothing.

"I'm afraid I can't find that title for sale anywhere."

"I knew you couldn't. You monsters."

Marcus had never tested the speed with which the police would respond to the panic button under the counter. He considered giving it a test run.

"Perhaps you could leave me your number and I could contact you if we ever get that title in," he said. "We're constantly acquiring new inventory."

The old man grunted, then wrote his name, number, and the title of the book on the slip of paper Marcus provided. Marcus slid it into the drawer under the counter. Without another word, the man turned and left the shop.

Marcus had more or less forgotten him by the time his next customer came through the door. Bookstores, especially used bookstores, attract all manner of eccentric. The old man was not the strangest patron he had encountered that week, or even that day.

A few weeks later, the man showed up again. Marcus only vaguely remembered him at first, but recalled him completely by the time he had finished his routine search and reached the point where he was asking to look through the rare books. When he had finished his perusal, Marcus noticed his eyes had welled up with tears. His body swayed slightly as he gripped a shelf to maintain his balance.

"I've been searching for that book for twenty years," he said. "I've hitchhiked around the country, haunting used bookstores, garage sales, estate sales. It's nowhere. Nowhere." He lowered his head. Marcus watched him in silence. After a moment, the man lifted his face and looked at Marcus through rheumy eyes. "I don't belong here. I want to go home."

Marcus felt a chill crawl up his spine.

The old man turned and faced the wall of books. He ran his fingers reverently across the spines of the regimented tomes. "All books are true," he said. He moved his arm in a broad gesture to indicate the mass of volumes around them. "There's not a single work of fiction in all these shelves. They aren't just books, they're worlds. You can travel to them and return from them in a never ending series of journeys." He turned to Marcus. "But those of your world have lost the capacity to travel to other realities. Like a beast with an atrophied organ. You no longer possess the ability to travel from one reality to the next. You read the pages of a book and imagine yourself to be in that world, but you've lost the capacity to leap into the pages. You could go anywhere you want. You could ride the backs of dragons or visit with Sherlock Holmes at 221B Baker Street. But all you do is imagine it. You never take the leap that would allow you to travel to those worlds."

He reached out and desperately grabbed Marcus.

"I was warned not to come. Yours is a forbidden world. But I had to see it. I had to witness the forbidden reality. You are the barbarians. You alone among the realities allow books to go out of print!" he shrieked.

"There are even legends that you burn books, you monsters!" He stumbled to the door and looked out the glass to the street above. "I can't stand it here! Do you have any idea how insipid people are who have only lived in one reality! When I arrived, I couldn't wait to leave, return to my own world." He turned to Marcus, his intense glare burning. "But I'm banished here, marooned more dreadfully than any cursed ancient mariner. You creatures allowed my book to go out of print! Of all the realities where I could have been imprisoned, I would give half my soul for it not to have been yours." He broke down crying, a wrenching cry, part despair, part alcohol, part madness.

"If what you say is true, why don't you just enter another book?" said Marcus, motioning to the shelves.

The old man looked at the silent volumes around him. "It's only possible to travel to another reality from your own. You have to return to your own world before you can jump off into another. Lateral moves between realities are impossible." He reached trembling fingers toward the shelves. "All these worlds, beckoning to me, taunting me. I've cried out to God to save me from this wretched place. Does your reality even *have* a God?! But in all the years of my existence here, my book has never surfaced."

He looked at Marcus with a gaze of despair and fear, as though he regretted the things he had revealed. He then turned and stumbled off into the night.

Marcus sat and watched the door for long minutes. Driven mostly by curiosity, he ran another internet search for the book. He could find no bookstores, no publishing warehouses, no estate sales that listed it. But he entered a request into all major databases. If the book appeared for sale anywhere in the country, he would be notified.

*   *   *

Marcus sat alone in the shop. It was an hour past closing. A sudden rattling of glass shook the silence. The old man stood at the door, yanking at the knob, trying desperately to open it. Marcus went to the door and unlocked it. The man burst through.

"You have it?" he groaned. "You really have it?"

"I do. It turned up at a small bookseller in the Midwest."

"Where is it?"

"Locked in the safe."

"Get it!" said the old man, desperately.

"Remain calm," said Marcus. "We haven't discussed the price."

The old man stared at him. "What do you want?" he croaked. "I'll steal for it. I'll kill for it."

"I don't want money," said Marcus. "I don't want you to commit any crimes or acts of violence. But I do have a price."

The old man listened as Marcus named his terms.

*   *   *

The shop was found open. There was a search, an investigation, but neither Marcus nor his strange customer were ever seen again.

After a time, Marcus' relatives acquired the contents of the store. A few of the rarer volumes were sold and scattered to various parts of the country.

The rest were sold for mulch.

Mark Pearce

guilty as charged –
kissing the gunner's daughter
without priming her

the gunner's daughter
matched me salvo for salvo
till our rounds were spent

combined fire-power
ensured this was more than just
a shot in the dark.

Bill Fitzsimons

Sweet Pauline
knew the real Doc Rickets
grew up on a chicken farm
outside of Yuba City
and she had to stand up in a line in Church
with the other kids
and say she was a sinner.
I am not, she thought quite firmly.

And after high school
which possibly she did not finish
when her father came to see her off
on the bus to San Francisco
and (his idea) they said a prayer together,
and he mentioned, once again, that
once you are saved, you are saved forever.
Oh Daddy, she wanted to tell him
(but hadn't the heart) *I never was saved at all*

In the city she started reading, for example
Carson McCullers
Karl Marx,
William Faulkner.
She met a furious minded married Communist
with a nice beard,
worked on the newspaper
got pregnant, couldn't go home again.

She and her son lived in
a house in Monterey
which was, it seemed, held together by its wall paper.
He cried and cried
with a long lasting fury he might have got from his beautiful
father.

She carried him along Cannery Row
to Pacific Grove
which was a dry town, Methodist,
to the popular liquor store
on the boundary
telling him about the
contradictory and interesting world

polyps and anemones
Democratic politics
and flocking birds and fishes,
trying to explain the civilizing thing
which is hard to use and beyond price.

Daniel Richardson

There was always a mystery about the gravedigger. He lived in a shack at the edge of the cemetery. In all his years in the town, he had made no friends. Some believed it was due to the natural aversion people have towards those of his profession; others believed it was a result of the mysterious nature of his arrival in town and the mystery of his past. No one knew where he came from or what he had done before arriving in Cleftville.

And now, he was dead. Among his effects were found papers identifying him as Jason Morgan, a notorious outlaw who had robbed the Morristown Bank twenty years earlier, then disappeared without a trace. Schoolboys had often hunted for the "Lost Treasure of Jason Morgan." And now it turned out he had lived among them for twenty years. Where could he have hidden it?

In a moment of epiphany, the townsfolk thought of the cemetery. For years, Morgan had been planting the deceased of Cleftville. What else might he have planted with them?

A fever overtook the town. Some rushed into the graveyard and began to dig with their fingers. Others took the time to dash home and return with shovels. There was no organizing principle. As they dug up a grave, they would push the coffin up onto the surface of the earth to check the soil beneath it, then they would jump out of the hole and drag the body half out of the coffin to see if there was gold in the coffin itself. Finding nothing, they would dash to the next grave and begin their frenzied digging anew.

It took hours, but eventually they desecrated every resting place in the cemetery. No treasure was found. In a sudden sheepish sobriety, unable to look each other in the eye, they slunk home, each to their own abode.

At well past midnight, an old vagabond came ambling down the road. He had been drifting in a more or less southerly direction for the past few weeks, sleeping in haylofts, riding the rails. The town of Cleftville was asleep as he passed through the graveyard.

In the dim light of the quarter moon, he could tell there was something wrong. He stopped in the midst of the cemetery and squinted his eyes all around. At that moment, the moon came from behind a cloud and the whole scene became clear. Every grave was open; every coffin lay askew beside its hole, and a body was halfway out of each coffin.

When the townsfolk arrived at the cemetery the next morning to undo the ravages of their debauch from the night before, they came across a mystery that they were never able to solve and which passed into the local town legend.

They counted three times, and came up with the same answer all three times. No one could explain it.

There were sixty-seven holes, but there were sixty-eight bodies.

Mark Pearce

Wild Buoys

PRUNING

The lavender is almost done,
spreads smoky pillows in the air,
storm-purpled spikes grow silver-grey,
cocoon perfume in grainy ears.

So is it time to gather in
the mellow summer-scented seed,
cut short the joy of butterflies,
the lazy buzz and bob of bees.

Sun benediction lingers on,
the season clings to shortening days
and who am I to bring an end
to this year's prayer for next year's praise.

Liz McPherson

GARDEN

A rabbit, worn and cloudy-eyed,
ears low, breath fogging,
lollops slowly among cabbage and spinach
beside the frosty hawthorn hedge,
boundary to a wide field.

He remembers summer, larking with his doe,
how they stumbled upon this plenteous land
in long warm dawns; how they laughed
when chased off, knowing the way
and time to return;

how they played and rolled
in secret hollows at the cool of dusk,
made love, raised kits, enough
for some to survive and go.

How the autumn day she disappeared
the wind howled and he smelled fox.

How it would soon be time for sleep.

William Coniston

FOX BODHISATTVA

Foxes appear, carrying the news, with all its lost aircraft and Circles of Hell. They carry the usual weather and sport, the celebrity fashion faux pas, but deep in their pelts they hold the births and deaths of oceans and distant nebulae. I haven't read Kerouac since my teens, but last night in the insistent jazz of windscreen wipers and passing lights, skin crackling like a million Dexedrine typewriters, I saw my reflection burning to its incandescent apotheosis. There are rats in the hedges and along the humming rail tracks, murmuring their soliloquies of milk, honey and endless garbage: there are foxes at the door, red as sleepless eyes, itching with the news no one wants to hear, dragging in the morning by its bleeding throat.

Oz Hardwick

She did not like
the idea of them
although they were
quite without venom
as I tried to explain
but she'd slipped away.
*

Never alive, just at the side of the road
where they have tried zebra-crossing,
leaving great holes in the wooded field edge.
*

The one he shot thinking it was a rabbit.
The one you hit with the car.

And those that leap
out from Egypt's
afterlife.
*

It came right up to our patio doors
and started attacking
the glass
                    an image
out of a rival poet's earth.
*

Clucking all the while you eat,
they cling to the walls, visibly
digesting a fly and now
one has flown on to your face.
*

Like a small bear
was how he described
what we decided
cannot have been
the creature we spotted
on the road to Glamis.
*

I saw the cop on our drive
with his gun out

but missed what he had followed

till it dragged its rabies
into our woodpile.
*
Whatever hibernation they have rolled into
still holds them and the noise of their
unimaginable love-making.
*
Like that character
on social media
who only rarely
risks poking out
his whiskers
to remark on
the flood.
*
Refugees, they hide out in the scrub
concealing ridge and furrow: one barks
and turns into a dog from that lost village.
*
A baby, he says,
as on the trail
ahead of us we see
a black smudge.
Maybe, I say,
but what about
its parents?
*
It can only have been a unicorn,
that creature cantering beside me
early one morning as I walked to work.

John Greening

endless hours of airport madness of coffee and wine and sugar and delays and security and fill out this form and taking your boots off and yes sir your belt too   and the hours are rolling and all sense tells you the planet still turns and your body tells you hours are passing as you see two in the afternoon for the third time in twenty-four hours   and it is not a hiccup there has not been a pause or a fracture or a skip it is you   it is you flying remorselessly into today as your friends back home get on with tomorrow it is you with your eyes stinging   your mind a fog of misremembering and unholy thoughts   your muscles heavy and your ageing back reluctant

at some point you look up and everyone is wearing Stetsons and shorts and there are so many youthful sunny dispositions and so many sturdy thighs and always there is a child screaming just out of view and a tired parent or two trying to dredge the last of their patience

a black cowboy with his black Stetson smiles and asks if I prefer bourbon to whisky   I say not if the whisky is good whisky and he smiles and says me too and falls back asleep again in the slumbering depths of his chair again

* * *

to the city where it rains and it rains and the sky unloads all that gathered Pacific as it crashes into those mountains and opens its palms and lets go of it all as if it were sin and evil thought in face of their redeemer   grey skies and coffee houses fire hydrants and confused intersections all stamped out in an enormous chequer-board grid and road manners from a different age   and the water runs down the sidewalks and the streets everyone has an umbrella and all the sad ambulances of British Columbia crash intersections whatever the lights are flashing   and the markets are grottoes bursting with fruit plump and fresh as jewels shining in every corner

there are bays so many tremendous welcoming bays and a False Creek and enormous high bridges that stride over all this water and all the while logs bump and bob hinting at some reptile past   old boats and old quays tumbledown shacks and tumbledown fishermen   and the great railway yards spreading like roots like ivy across this enormous land   all this railroad Earth and what I wouldnt give for a sunflower this morning

Nick Allen

OUR EYES

then told us straight,
that Gorgons were
no more – yet our
fingers couldn't feel
old Nessy's lost
conclusion,
and the
Yeti remained too
unscented. But

now we do taste
the fear of the dog;
new big cats are in town –
they're monsters
of futures of
shivers robotic –
and so darkness
nevermore unnerves him

as he stands
in twenty forty-five.

Mandi Lynsdale

Given that it was out of season, she found Mars delightful
on that first visit. Finding nothing open
didn't bother her. She didn't need the casino,
the bars, the chippies or the nail parlours,
and a week without a lot of chattering company
was a welcome prospect. She was content wandering
in the ambient red light, sitting from time to time
to listen to a soothing voice read the latest
AI rewrite of *Pride and Prejudice,* enjoying
it most when she changed the voice setting
to *female/English/Berkshire.* By the Tuesday,
she was walking more strongly, recognising
by sight some of the other people around,
feeling comfortable. So it came as a shock
when, on her Thursday walk well beyond
the edge of town, she turned to see on the sand,
half sunk, the shattered remains of a spaceship,
twenty-first century, covered in teethmarks.

Rod Whitworth

A dream had been reported in Outer Sector B7. It's desolate and dangerous out there—buildings smithereened from recent bombardments, girders and roofs askew ready to drop deadly. We got some samples—birdsong, buttercups in grass, children at play—but lost traces before we could stream them back to HQ. They're always saying, You can't have a dream without a dreamer, blah blah. But no-one's gonna step out of the dust and shadows and volunteer theirselves are they, unless Hey it was me, sorry for the inconvenience, bang.

Then we started picking up very different signals. At first we thought it was just old-style imagination. Elly said it was dream and she was right, but the code was different, it didn't match the other, and HQ hadn't picked it up. We got a circling raptor, a cliff from below then above—classic scene-fade—sense of imminence, silent scream. Nothing new there. But we couldn't go back with two unresolveds, and we were shit-scared we'd been lured. Duleep was trying to mash them together convincingly on the system, but there was an imagination gap. We were looking in the wrong way—scanning waves and vibrations but not seeing with sight. Stepping through rubble—bricks, plaster, timber, dust, bones, rags—I stood back against a wall to view as much as I could from shade. Elly came up, squinting — What's that? —looking just beyond my shoulder. I turned as her pointing drew our focus to some marks. It had been an interior wall. Scratched on grey plaster were two imitations, representations, of humans, lines carved on the surface with intent—two figures, one apparently leaning on the other. She said it's what was called depiction. Humans represented by humans? Spooky. We had what we needed, scanned and streamed it back, got the hell out of there.

Kevin Armor Harris

Vinyl spins –
a classic love song crackling through the speakers,
and in the middle of the crowd,
a woman sways in memory.
She's clothed in stains of baby spit
cups of tea at the PTA, jelly cups,
side-eye glances on the edge of the playground.
Daddy's gone to get ice lollies from the van.
Once, she wore heels like daggers
and moved like a firefly
through velvet-lit clubs.
Now she dances in trainers on the high street,
a dandelion tucked behind her ear,
a ring on her thumb, laughter on her lips.
The baby in her arms gazes at her;
she is his whole world.
Her older kid pulls at her jumper:
Mum, you're dancing weird. People are looking.
She smiles at him, tousles his hair.
Weird is what keeps us alive.

Lauren K Nixon

Before the corporate spaces that came initialled
NEC, O2, Bet 365
bands too big for town halls and their Cuban boots
would sort out cavernous spaces
to ply their trades.

I saw the Stones in a Leicester Roller skating rink,
I'm told The Beatles played a Shrewsbury Cinema
and in Stafford, we had Bingley Hall Agricultural Showground.
Between Dairy Shows and County Fairs
Fleetwood Mac trailered in their Californian magic
To sadly dissipate in this cattle market;
bass and drums echoing the agricultural hangar.
My Dream woman Stevie Nicks disappeared
into a midlands indoor cattle market
and down my top ten, rosette taken back
despite her change of shawls and head bands.

Bob Marley played there twice;
The first with a whiff of horse muck in the air.
Strange sweet smells to rhythms so heavy
the concrete pillars managed
to bounce to the beat without breaking
while the pointed elbows   of the crazy white guy
                      in front of me
danced out of time with both the music and the beams.

The second time he played
Bob Marley was ill looked like his own ghost.
We knew he was dying
The car park emptied quietly.
We followed each other out
As orderly   as   sheep.

Steve Harrison

in a field, tent-pegging the ground
into long corridors of sheep-soiled
hand-burning nylon rope,

then sauntering up and down
in studied slowness, shoving
a cart something like a pushchair

as its radar penetrates the earth,
reflects what look like random waves
back to its small screen?

The hope is, once home, the software
will develop, like a black and white photo;
revealing features, puzzles to be solved.

All further clues are buried,
informed inferences unavailable,
inaccessible without a dig.

So we let imagination fly:
that line might be a road, wall,
not a water pipe at all;

that blob with possible corners
could be a rare square barrow
not a rubble heap.

We ignore Occam's razor,
indulge in theories without limits,
the bliss of knowing ignorance;
until ground is broken,
truth revealed, bubble burst.

Ann Gibson

GREAT APE

Caught in his unblinking stare
beneath feral parakeets bawling their green
through the canopy, eye the gorilla's graven image.
Beyond him, shadows blotch a tarmac path
from AdventureLand! to the Victorian bandstand
where tatterdemalions rage and quaff all day.
Water gathers a crowd to dabbling beaks.
Park keepers stab litter in its drifts,
while someone's blue, oblique balloon
rises to a heartbreak sky. Immobile as
his relentlessly petted head, the silverback's
plastic shame frames the growing queue for Krayzee Golf.
Fingers poke the shadow organs of his sense.
He blanks in every selfie.

Craig Dobson

MARION LIVSEY (1924-1970)

Say, you chose drowning
                                        as a more poetic way to go.
Say, the smell of lilies
                                didn't linger on the windowsill
like the memory of old musk.

Say, you put on your heels
                                        and tap-danced downstairs.

Say, you were drawn
                                to the glowing light of the refrigerator.
Say, a glass of water
                                dripped down your throat
like a baptism.

Say, there were no monsters
                                        no memory of fire.

Say, your daughter was sleeping
                                                peacefully, in the next room.
Say, it wasn't your time.

Say, you were already home.

Eve Chancellor

Even as I take the first step into what used to be your garden, I am furious. Branches whip at my face, bushes block my path, and uneven paving slabs trip me underfoot. It smells of dirt and rot and leaf mulch covers the ground all around me. My nice shoes are already ruined.

You've left me to sort out your mess. Again. You bloody did this to me, your own sister.

Selfish.

Didn't you realise I have my own life to live? I'm busy enough without having to clean up and sell off your rickety old house in the middle of nowhere. In the middle of Winter, too, when the housing market is at its quietest.

Luckily, I've found people willing to sort out the interior – for a price, of course. They're already clearing out your tat, and they'll give it a deep clean afterwards.

But nobody will go near your garden, not in this state. When I sent photos, every single person told me no. Even Henry – who you hate, of course – told me to do it myself.

So it's down to me. As always. I'm the one you're punishing with this mess. Your mess. The last mess of yours I'll ever have to sort out, thank goodness.

I've carved a month out of my schedule, between contracts, so I'm here. Tidying up this damn garden, every day, until it's over and I've sold the house.

Why'd you have to go and kill yourself, sister? Why'd you have to die so suddenly?

* * *

I've found a box of tools in the shed. They're all rusting and the shed door only half opened because of the bloody holly bush, but I do have tools now. I can get started.

I found your gardening gloves in the box. They're crusting, stiff from years of use, but they fit my hands. Unsurprisingly, I suppose, since I have the same hands as you.

You'd always make me hold my hand up to yours when we were kids, to compare the sizes.

'To make sure you aren't growing up faster than me,' you'd say.

You read my palms a couple of years ago. I pouted the whole time, wanting to leave, but you wouldn't take no for an answer. That was the last time you did that thing, with our hands.

You said my Heart Line was deep and long and I rolled my eyes.

I did grow up faster than you, in the end. And our hands will never touch again.

But the gloves do fit. That, at least, hasn't changed.

* * *

I'm starting with the bushes, mainly because they're the biggest problem. Henry always tells me I'm the sort of person to start with the hardest task, and he loves me for it.

I'm sure you wouldn't agree with him. Even if you did think the same, you'd disagree purely because Henry said it.

You never made it easy for me, you know, when you treated him like that. Glaring at him, always arguing. It pushed us apart. I had to side with my husband, how could I not?

Anyway, the bushes. I'm glad I brought Henry's chainsaw because you don't seem to have one – or any electrical equipment, for that matter.

Even from the grave, you're managing to make my life awkward. If nothing else, you're consistent.

* * *

The chainsaw only worked for two minutes before it squealed, spluttered, and went silent. Now it won't turn on.

I've resorted to using these long scissors I found in your toolbox. Shears, maybe? I don't know the name.

I tried to listen to a podcast, but my headphones aren't working and I've no bloody signal either. I've just been chopping away at these bushes in silence. It's excruciating.

I'm covered in scratches already and I can't feel my fingers or toes, even though I'm somehow also sweating buckets. My lips are cracked, my arms are throbbing, and I've only managed a single bush. I've even scratched my bloody watch, the one Henry bought for me. It's expensive and beautiful and your garden broke it. I can just imagine you laughing at my struggles.

Or maybe you wouldn't be laughing. Maybe you'd say in your stupid sincere voice that gardening is meditative, that I'm cleansing my soul by being close to nature. Some utter tosh like that.

You'd probably give me a crystal, too. I'm surprised I haven't found one tied to a tree.

I did find a patch of sage, though, buried under a bush. I bet you used to pick that and burn it, to 'purify your space' or whatever. You always talked about sage like it was magical but this plant was wilting, nearly dead.

It's back in the sun now. Maybe it will live in spite of you.

* * *

I don't understand why you let the garden get so overgrown. This was your haven. On those rare occasions we did talk, you never stopped going on about it – your new bushes, the plants you were propagating, the birdhouse you'd built by hand.

I found the birdhouse on the floor. It was on its side, the roof split open, and woodlice were living inside. Fragments of wood were scattered everywhere. When I cleared it up, splinters pricked me through your gloves.

I've found a frisbee we used to play with as kids, too. It was lost at the back of the garden, covered in grime. A worm was crawling over it.

I washed it with the hose and have been throwing it up and down the garden – collecting it myself, since nobody is here to throw it back. There's a princess on it, faded but still smiling. You used to say she looked like me.

You put so much thought into that birdhouse, but then you let it break. I don't understand why you stopped caring about these things.

You didn't tell me you needed help with the garden. I could have found someone to help. I could have done something.

You never asked.

But, then again, I never really gave you a chance.

* * *

I'm building up a pile of clutter on the lawn. When I'm done, I'll have a bonfire, like the ones Dad used to have when we were kids. You were always scared of them. You'd make him check the pile for hedgehogs before he set it alight. I liked watching the flames dance.

Maybe my bonfire will smell of lavender, or sage or sap or something. I've found some nice smells since I started here. Under the stench of rot.

* * *

I think I might move into your spare bedroom, now that the men have cleared it out. Just temporarily. It'll save money, not having to stay in a hotel any more, and it'll be more efficient if I don't have to travel every day.

The hotel staff have been glaring at my arms, too, all battered and bruised from my fight with this place. And I keep finding twigs in my hair.

I can't seem to shake the smell of dirt from myself. You're turning me into you, I swear. I've never been such a mess.

* * *

We share a taste in flowers, I'm realising, now that I've cleared the bushes. Perennials, mostly: plants that last.

I think I'll leave the flowers as they are, assuming they've survived being buried alive. I certainly can't get rid of them all. An empty garden is even worse than a messy one. An empty garden is sad to look at.

You'd have probably found a deeper meaning in that, claiming it's a metaphor for our lives. You always did things like that.

I'm just talking about gardens, though, nothing more. I don't think like you. I never have.

* * *

The bushes are finally sorted, now onto the trees. I've started with the one by the back door – a cherry blossom, I think. I remember visiting you once when this place was still tidy, maybe three years ago. It was covered in delicate pink flowers. One got stuck in my hair.

I can't tell if the tree is still alive. It's lost its leaves but then that's what happens in Winter. Even if it is dead, it's giving me a good fight. My face is bleeding from one of its cuts.

Henry found the time to visit but he just criticised everything. The bushes aren't neat enough, apparently, and the flowers aren't right. Especially the ones I planted.

I just let him grumble, it's easier that way.

I won't change your garden for him, don't worry. I wouldn't do that to you.

He gave me back my watch. The glare that came off it was blinding so I've stuffed it in the bottom of one of my bags. In your garden, I prefer to lose track of time.

Henry fixed the chainsaw when he was here but it broke again as soon as I tried to use it. There's something about your garden that it can't handle.

* * *

I took a break from the trees because I had a sudden urge to do the weeding. After I'd finished, I realised just how like you that was – following a whim, not thinking logically.

It's looking so much better, good enough that I can imagine how it will look when it's sorted out: not quite what it was when you were alive, but still okay. I even caught myself daydreaming about flowers I could buy for the beds.

I watered the herbs today, now that I've uncovered them. I might be imagining it, but the sage looks much happier.

* * *

Should I have realised that something was wrong? Did something push you over the edge, something you didn't tell me about? I can't fathom what it might have been, to make you do something so awful. I can't imagine doing what you did. It makes my skin crawl.

We'd barely spoken for months. The last time I saw you was on my birthday, when you came round to give me a card. I invited you in, I think, but Henry called out from somewhere in the house and you said you couldn't stay.

You did look gaunt. There were bags under your eyes, and your smile seemed forced. I just assumed you didn't want to see me. I never thought there was something else going on.

I rarely ever thought about you, in fact. You were just a fixture of my life, like a load-bearing wall. I never considered the weight you were carrying.

* * *

I've found a box full of scrapbooks in your spare room. There are so many photos of me, of us. Of our parents.

I opened the last one, which was unfinished.

Why didn't you tell me how much you were struggling? Why didn't you call me? I could've helped to declutter your mess. I could've done something. Didn't you know that's what sisters are for?

I guess I do know why you didn't call. I just don't want to admit it.

If you called, I probably wouldn't have answered.

* * *

I burned the pile of branches and leaves, like I said I would, and I watched as the flames rose above the tallest tree. Before long, there was just a pile of ash, a patch of black where I'd killed the grass.

It didn't smell of sweet things, like I thought it might. It smelled of smoke. Obviously. Why did I ever think fire would smell of anything else?

I did check for hedgehogs before I set it alight, though. I managed that much, at least.

* * *

And now it's done. The bushes are neat, the trees trimmed, the plants blooming. And I've reseeded the lawn, too.

I've picked some of the sage, now that it's showing signs of life, and I'm going to burn it. I'll purify your garden in the way you would have done.

I will cleanse it of my stagnant presence and sell the house. Then, when Spring comes again, the cherry blossom will fall on someone else's head.

George Burnett

Untitled

The outgoing winds of my descent
  Storm, they bluster the night-blue sky.
  Yet circumspect I tread and lie
About my age. I did not invent

The sails or the trumpets 'fanfare,
  Nor was I present at the muster
  That later stormed the hereafter.
I was lost, like scent upon the air,

And could not know and thus not find
  The place from where the winds are summoned
  And blast us home towards our end.
I've often dreamed I could rewind

The wind, unmake the tug of years,
  And hear the silence that would reign
  Over the eerie, deathless plain.
But the wind blows and one always hears.

Leo Shearmur

LITTLE SABLE POINT

The palm of a dune
holds us up to the
night sky to watch
shooting stars, and
we try not to make
wishes we'll regret
as we instinctively
duck our heads each
time the lighthouse
beam sweeps over
us and our fingers
tunnel toward each
other, hissing through
the sand and fusing
into fulgerites.

Kyle Heger

So, anyway, I'm walking back from the pub.
It's the hottest day of the year.
Brazil has just beaten Serbia, 2-1,
and I've sat on the front with the crossword
looking up at times to watch the sun go down
and between the houses I see the full moon
over the railway bridge, past the playground.

No children, just three wild rabbits,
and one starts chasing another
round the roundabout, round and round,
then the other one turns round,
and chases the chaser the other way.

And I send you a text, share the moment,
drop a stone into a bottomless well.

Stuart Handysides

GENEALOGY

I tumbled from impractical stock.
Great-grandfather stumbled
on a platform in the rain,
raddled the wheels of an oncoming train.

Grandfather lost the use of an arm
trying to fix a toaster.
Jammed a knife in till his palm clammed shut,
frying the nerves to his shoulder.

Father fell from a pier one holiday,
slipped on some dropped ice cream.
Bobbed up, dead, at a beauty spot,
mangled by the props of a superyacht.

Mindful of my ancestors, I move cautiously.
Don't travel on or tinker with machinery.
Stay clear of heights and away from the sea.
Won't take the stabilizers off my son's bike;

never so much as dandle him on my knee.

Craig Dobson

A geologist details your lineage
    and strata. The exposition is long.
The evening sun warms your salterella grits,
    turns each peak white as any sugar daddy,
exposes the lines of disruption running deep.
    Remember the Torridonian times? The bands?
Hornblende. Conglomeritic. The planet rocked
    to your metamorphic events. There were rumours.

Cross-bedding, acid gneiss with alluvial fans,
    tales of fantastic pinnacles, trips down
vertical worm burrows, pipes with serpulites,
    talc-and-tremolite schists. Then came the break ups.
Sediment piled up. Massive crystalline dolomites
    set into a grey matrix while you wrestled
with a belt of complication and that transgression
    in the Cambrian quartzite, the omicron type after-bed.

Your schists became flaggy and silaceous.
    There was still some rude foliation, occasional
orogenic events in the Moines. Now
    its gentle folds among the relict Mountains,
your terraces deformed by areas of denudation,
    erratic outcrops. You might rumble out
the odd landslide, but basically its long dip slopes
    all the way to the end of the anthropocene.

Sue Butler

SMOOTH NEWT

for months we have been hidden
from each other   lumbering   slumbrous

now your back flip
        like the whoosh
of last years grassheads
        into the skip

shucks off winter   a small rush of air
barely there   the breath of the piper
before the tune
        and your splash
        somersaults us into Spring

you chassé
        through the cream striped iris spears
sway among the lily pads
        earth scuffed belly crawler no more
in the water's embrace   you flash
        your tangerine courting suit
            and dance

Sue Butler

HURT CROW

Female, probably – brown bar above the beak – one wing
is raggedy, curtailed: hop, flutter, hop –
spry, growing, fed by well-wishers. Home is here,

this lawn, between Church Hall and road: you watch
– lorries dinning by – the bench people,
keeping well back; jump-flutter through the fence

to the small stream. Years ago – Cape Town –
a footless sparrow – café bird: on delicate splinters, poised,
it beaked up crumbs. – Here, we tilt away

from the long light. – And when the North wind blows? –
shivering groundling – some shrub, hole,
a shed? – you are too wild and quick – you raggle-taggle –

to catch. Eat, eat: do you sense the bleak
approaching cold? Brilliant berries load the rowans,
hollies. Now you are mettlesome with protein –

should that be? ... *not one of them will fall to the ground
unperceived*... What does the universe want? – frail
crumbled bones? a broth of a bird, but broken, iron-earth-bound?

Vuyelwa Carlin

(Lines 16-17: Matthew 10.29: *Are not two sparrows sold for a penny? Yet not
one of them will fall*
to *the ground unperceived by your Father.)*

who scythes the miles,
screeching, sleeping
on the wing, long curve
towards a small hole
under the eaves
and, finding it filled,
arcs away without pause
as if she had not invested
the whole ocean in it

Elaine Ewart

it's like an injured animal, my heart
snagged red in the trap's mouth,
& I don't know how to spring the latch –
I thrash, twist, pivot,
which I believe in enlightened circles is known as resistance,
as in: *you're too fastened to the world, and the stories which inhabit it*,
& perhaps it's true, like a hunger,
I've accumulated years over clear sight,
as my mum was keen to impress: *they can't bury you with it*,
but who are *they* & what is *it*,
& what if bleeding out is how I hear my own voice, like:
I can't picture a moon I don't belong to,
a purple field I won't run through,
a lover's hide I won't return to,
even if they cause me to suffer, I still want it, the trap,
perhaps some of us can't be helped,
but endure like a love song,
cherry mouth prized open

Alex Rourke

SAID THE TRAPPER TO THE BIRD
after The Larsen Magpie Trap

Think of it as a kind of therapy.
This is the best room we offer
and for you

    it's free.

See how sky is rectangled
within wire, the space airy, well-lit,
distractions visible yet entirely

    beyond reach.

Climb the sides of the cage,
skitter from perch to perch,
turn in livid purple circles.

    Will you be released?

I understand your need to ask the question.
A good conclusion to our first session is key.
For now, I'll leave you
              pecking.

    Trust me.

Catherine Glavina

Hands of the willow hang idle in the courtyard
but the House
is prayers and rules and bells and walls
and names scratched into walls.

Is your name in the register of inmates.
Drift of your scissored hair to the floor's clean slate.
An ache swelling finger-joints hour after hour
after hour unpicking tarred hemp

or granulating animal bones with an iron bar.
Is never being taught to read or write.
Is three meals a day, weighed and measured,
with a snatch of bread thrown over the wall
to your husband. And the punishment for that.

*

The seven classes of indigent comprise
the able-bodied and the infirm poor,
the old, the mentally ill, the vagrant,
orphans and unwed mothers.
These last wear a short blue jacket
and at Christmas go without the dinner.

*

In the gap in the wall, a silhouette
of swans and spades and scythes and stooks of barley
bulrushes with a heron at the ready
and two teams of Suffolks ploughing head to head.
Wrought iron gates. The locked impossible country.

*

They take their ease, the workhouse dead,
under grass in the hollow where clay was dug
for workhouse bricks. No plaque. No stone.
Orchard rows for memorial.
Pine Apple Russet. Hubbards Pearmain.
Summer Broaden. Winter Majetin.

Patrick Yarker

Was thirty dollars
In our mailbox
Got us through
In that sickly pea
Green upstairs flat
With the broken steps
Bread milk hamburger
More than just one
Can of lima beans
In the ready to fall
Off the wall cupboard
For my little sister and I
Until Dad's next
Big-big-all-but-done
Deal came along
Dad said it was
Gary the nice guy
With the thick black
Glasses and shaky hands
At the photo counter
Rexall Drug downtown
Who once drank
Married to Kay
(Who always seemed
Too gaunt too worried)
Who'd lend a hand
To anyone he could
Whenever he could
Wasn't the money
That got us through
Was the kindness
Was that simple

David Sapp

LEAF TAO
(after Derek Mahon's The Mayo Tao)

'I have been working for years
on a four-line poem
about the life of a leaf ... '

thought, scrolled, bud, cold;
open, green, fragile, fresh;
plenitude of golden sun;
dry, crinkled, russet, gone.

Philip Dunkerley

creeping forget-me-not   needy as ever   purple loosestrife   what a
gal!
    jack in the hedge   probably innocent   best not loiter though
buttercup   a cow   yellow cow   jersey cow   not butter   nor cup
    bog myrtle   tomboy   look at those socks   go wash those hands
devilsbit scabious   could be catching   best not get too close
    timothy upright   suit   tie   never recovered from school bullying
hoary ragwort   give a wide berth   there's gossip
    lesser / greater burdock   let them slug it out
herb robert   wasn't he the boy ... didn't they own the corner shop
    perennial honesty   no-one is that good
dandelion   a bit too wizard of oz   not just yellow brick roads but
tarmac
    any crack of opportunity for shaking that fuzzy head
parachuting offspring into world domination
    prickly poppy and touch-me-not-balsam   for a quiet life leave them
to it

Eve Jackson

Charles Rennie Mackintosh
might have liked
the marquetry
of its polished copper
and mahogany thorax,
the ten
precisely placed white squares
that border its wing-covers,
the surprise
of bright yellow knee-warmers
on long-stick legs.

A little research -
It's a leaf-footed Canadian
Western Conifer-seed
Bug, a pest
of timber plantations,
reportable
to the GB Non-native Invasive Species
Secretariat. As requested,
l will send them its portrait,
but then I'll free it
to find a pine, a spruce, a cedar.

Emmaline O'Dowd

Mayflies in the dying light:
they strut and pose
adopt grand gestures
for their magic devices,
for their "Instant Grams".
I have seen them come and go;
brief flashes against the sun.
I have hung for six hundred years
in the great hall, in oils,
in person, in spirit.
I will outstay them all.

Ali Pardoe

it was getting late when you messaged:
aurora, as if alluding to an elusive code
like rosebud or argo, then came a video:
a nocturnal-grained shower of pixels
flared over the rooftops of our beloved city
like an invite to share in the same different sky
we were both alone under, only,
outside all I found was monday night –
starless, light pollution, dead – *where?*
I replied, and you laughter-cried emoji
and shot back: *look through your camera!*
pink saturn rings, ecstatic green glimmers
invisible to the eye, made supernatural, alive
like the sci-fi film of my life,
I lowered my phone: loss, dark,
then raised it again: alive, & for a time
I felt the atlantic squeeze between us
via a second sight I didn't dare lower

Alex Rourke

We pick up our pencils. *Look.*
Thin clipped black hairs
point lines of iron filings straight
down the slope of your skull.
Hawk eyes under tufted brows
observe us as we sketch.
Stay with the image.

Speech alters the shape
of cheeks, but *lots of trembling
edges are good.* Your smile
fades, melancholy in repose.
I can't get the hang of
your jumper folding zigzags
where your stomach fails to bulge.

Hands tuck, right over left,
legs crossed otherwise.
Have you left room for the feet?
Everyone sighs. *Look at what's wrong
and put it right.* Impatient, the sun
throws your shadow against the wall, and
executes it faultlessly.

Sue Norton

She finds she's in new country every day,
though this is home and here's the heart of it,
where, while she works, her changeful daughter plays -
her cluttered studio, where they live and eat.
She'd thought to be a mother, she would slay
herself as artist, but she's saved both selves -
she's made the child her subject: neatly piled
in drawings, paintings, sculptures on the shelves,
the captured baby time had tried to steal.
And soon she'll catch the toddler, then the child,
the teenage girl. As far as she can tell,
she gives her all that makes a rounded human.
It's work in progress, and if things go well,
her masterpiece will be a living woman.

Emmaline O'Dowd

Untitled

I'M SENDING YOU AN AIRMAIL
After Stav Poleg

Inside, you'll find the collected works
of Jeffery Deaver, the road from Holmfirth
covered in deep deep snow, the Yorkshire
Sculpture Park – Henry Moore, Barbara Hepworth
and all the sculptors since, the heat of Aigues-Mortes
after a long ride in Provençal sun, Joni Mitchell
with her big yellow taxi, the back seat of a tandem,
Rembrandt's etchings, 23 polaroid cameras, a tub
of Rodda's Cornish Clotted and a strawberry
to go with it, the confidence to know how
good you are. I've sent it recorded delivery.

Rod Whitworth

How Did He Do That?

How do you know when you meet one,
one of the good ones?
The rule is, some people say,
you don't notice anything exactly but
you get a sort of unusual
floating feeling
and carried along feeling
like a leaf on a stream, let's say,
and some sense
of an incursion
of ongoing unreality,
although each thing and event is joined to the next,
but it doesn't really
take the centre of your attention

until a special moment,
hard to define,
but quite definite
just
afterwards
when it's finished

and, let's say, you feel a chill,
you pat for your reassuring wallet
and find you don't
actually, even, any more
possess trousers.

Daniel Richardson

What crime had I committed to have brought my father back
from the dead last night to solemnly confront me?
I am not Prince Hamlet etc. But he'd found,
he said, my secret vessel and then showed it to me:
incriminating enough for his friends to be looking on
in silence as he swung wide the shed door.

Is this because of that sudden news about the King
(my father's name was Charles) and how he'd not concealed
his diagnosis? It's curious we even have a king,
as curious as that Alice in Wonderland word itself
with all its Dickensian clutter, its sentimental half-
truth and double meaning, a well we reach into.

Usually my dreams go skiing, enjoy
an exhilarating free run down above
any buried snags but last night I knew there was
something, more than that boat in the shed, something I must
confess to or it would start eating away
but if I did before I woke is still unclear.

John Greening

The air on the ward is saturated with the sounds and smells of need. The phone's been ringing in vain since I came on shift. The dinner trolley has just arrived and wafts a reminder of the woman in Bed 18 who can't find her mouth and needs my help to eat. Beep, beep, beep, Bed 25's infusion line is blocked – again. A smell of shit is coming from behind the curtains of the man in Bed 3, who I left on the commode ten, twenty, minutes ago. The muted staccato of an unanswered bedside call bell pulses its slow heartbeat, as if time is running out. Someone who's past the point of comprehending how a call bell works – or has given up waiting – is shouting for help.

'Do you think I could possibly get back into bed now?' the man in Bed 4 asks my back as I'm half out the door of his bay, 'I've been sat here since this morning. My hip hurts, and I'm so cold'.

I turn to face him, quickly scanning the collection of symbols on the magnetic board above his bed – falls-risk, diabetic, not for resuscitation – that makes us think we know him.

'Ah, I'm really sorry to hear that,' I say – and I do mean it, but the man on the commode and the lady who can't eat her dinner and the anonymous cry for help and the man in Bed 2 opposite – who's supposed to always have someone with him in case he tries to stand and falls again and is now shuffling his bum towards the edge of his seat – are nosily jostling my brain.

The thin man in Bed 4 who's sat clenched in pain has gentle blue eyes and thick white hair that hasn't been combed today. He's wearing the hospital-issue mint pyjamas whose sleeves and legs are always either too long or too short: the uniform of patients who don't have anyone in their life keeping a vigil over them with a supply of their own clean clothes. He's clinging tight to the wooden armrests of his chair, as if he were sitting on a rough sea rather than solid ground. I wonder how many times he's watched me come into his bay and deal with other people's needs.

The way he asked if he could get into bed so quietly and to my back and the way he's now looking at me, searching my face as if for something to hold on to, cuts a space into the crowd of other people filling my head. 'I wish you'd asked for help sooner,' I say softly, stepping closer, 'and not sat there in discomfort all this time.' But even as I speak the words, I know they belong in another reality I wish existed, not the one he's landed into, where requests that aren't urgent from those with kind eyes are drowned in the cacophony of claims on never enough time.

'I was told I had to sit out here. I didn't want to,' he offers by way of explanation. 'I assumed I had to wait until someone came and put me back.' He says this so matter-of-factly and without complaint that it catches my heart. I see the scenario clearly; a nurse ten hours into a twelve-hour shift – her fourth in a row – is standing over him as he lies in his too-short mint pyjamas that belonged to someone else last week; she's run out of capacity for explanation or reassurance and her brusqueness is enough to exile him from himself. There's no magnetic symbol to alert us that this gentleman will do anything to avoid making a fuss.

I perch on the edge of his bed so my eyes are at his level, 'It's always *your* choice,' I tell him with a forcefulness that surprises me. 'It's your choice whether you sit out in the chair. And it's your choice how long you stay there. Don't ever forget that.'

'Really?' he asks simply.

'It is your choice,' I repeat, reaching out to touch his left hand, which has managed to unmoor itself from its grip on the armrest and is hovering in front of him. 'I'll go and get some help now.' The likelihood of me finding someone else who's free to help me any time soon is zero. But he's sitting up a little straighter in his chair, and I don't want to crush whatever it is that's returning to him by telling him this.

I spot the man in Bed 4's nurse hurrying down the corridor outside and follow after her. 'Can you help me?' I call out.

She stops and turns towards me, but her feet are still pointing in the direction of the beeping blocked infusion three bays away. I explain how the man in Bed 4 has been stuck out in his chair and is in pain and needs to be hoisted back into bed. But what I want more than anything is for her to know that he's been like this for hours because he thought he had to be. What I want more than anything is for all the quiet, easily-invisible souls not to be voiceless, here on the ward – anywhere.

'I'll get there as soon as I can,' she says flatly.

'Can you also document in his handover notes that he didn't tell anyone, so it doesn't happen again?' I call after her as the beeping pulls her on down the corridor towards her impossible to-do list. She doesn't answer; I know there's no room in her for my plea because she has a hundred others already backed up, like the last person trying to squeeze into a rush-hour tube that the other passengers simply can't make room for.

I can't find anyone else on the ward who's not already busy with another patient. I return to the man in Bed 4 and carefully wrap a blanket around his immobile legs. I tell him I've asked for help to get him back into his bed, and that it may take a little while. 'But' – I can tell it's essential he knows – 'I promise I won't forget about you.'

'Thank you,' he says, pausing before finding the courage to add something else, 'It's the first time anyone's listened to me since I got here.'

And it seems to me – as I hold his gaze and tuck his blanket a little tighter – that whether or not he gets any respite from his coldness and pain soon, what matters most right now is this.

Sarah Thorne

Charlotte phones as I step through the door and I can tell from the tightness of her voice she's seen the new biopic. I drop the shopping on the kitchen table, shoulder the screen to my ear. *It's a travesty*, Charlotte fumes. *So I'm a monster, sacrificing my siblings on the altar of my ambition? I'm sick of being Least Favourite Sister. Who'd remember them at all, if it wasn't for me?* I hear her angry breathing as I empty a pack of spaghetti into the pot. *It's just a phase.* She insists, *I'm being punished for surviving.* I remind her she's lived down scandals before. How her fulsome dedication to Thackeray in *Jane Eyre* started a rumour she was sleeping with him. *Oh God*, she groans, *I did drop a brick. How was I to know his wife was in an asylum?* Above the rattle of the kettle coming to the boil, she tells me, *I wrote an essay on fame, once. Back when I was quite clueless.* I ask, *Was that in Brussels?* There's a pause, and as I close the microwave door on the meatballs, I know she's thinking of her Professor. No point telling her to let that go. I describe to Charlotte my favourite scenes from *Villette*: the drugged walk in the park; Lucy burying Dr John's letters; Lucy handing M. Paul the noose of cotton. I know my devotion is not enough. The signal drops for a moment, and then I hear, *Their dogs, you know. When I got home from Scarborough. Dashing round me in circles when I opened the front door.* I say, *Char, I've got to go. Look, forget that film.* She says, *I've forgotten already.* Her tone has softened. Though I don't believe her, the words acknowledge me, like a sword brought down on my shoulder as I kneel.

Elaine Ewart

You Need New Shoes

I know you're there, love.
Those brown shoes tap music
like they did at our wedding.
Except now, they have impatient soles
that want to hurry me up.

You never used to be so thirsty
for the hours and minutes.
It's like they're leaving the world
through this door and we're trying
to catch them.

And anyway love, why does this door
never lead to a holiday?
I wake up with my flight ticket, but we
never manage to check in. Book the taxi,
instead of walking those shoes to the pub −

let's see where else the beer flows.
I'd rather not taste another early night
and have you spend days
tucked up on the sofa. Alone
with those shoes.

Shoes that know our story
seem to fall apart, like we do.
It's time new life walked in.

Julie Stevens

HAIRCUT EPITHALAMIUM

Conspicuously missing
My old bones
Couldn't quite get
To my son's wedding
However as the occasional
Soothsayer I knew
The nuptials were certain
And began to compose
My intended epithalamium
The summer before

The augury wasn't a predictable
Demonstration of courtship
It wasn't when
They stole morsels
From each other's plates
It wasn't when
They curled up on
The couch as young
Lovers are wont to do
Forming that single multi
Limbed mythical creature

It was a haircut
She sat him in
A chair in the yard
And draped a towel
Around his shoulders
My son bowed his head
Blissfully a boy again
Surrendering to her scissors
Her precise decisions

David Sapp

DECONSTRUCTING

Today we sit
in Booths
and there's
a gap in your head.
I don't
understand how
they can keep
taking pieces.
You smile
and there's
another tooth
gone. Last week
they told us
they're taking
your lips.
They'll stretch
them into
 a rictus when
the cancer's
dug out,
sew them
shut. I'm trying
to cling
onto you
but pretty soon
there'll be
nothing
left.

Liz McPherson

MIRROR

I put the mirror up to his lips
a little pink plastic-rimmed oval
which used to be attached to a folding hairbrush
clamshell style
and came with a purchase of tampons
decades ago
a female gift

I hold it close in front of his lips
when there seems to be no more rise and fall
however slight, of his failing chest
and no longer any sound at all

I lift it, look
the mirror is clear

Something between stars and hands
or small birds' feet

yellow leaves
flat on the flagstones
seem to be pointing their way
towards me

making for inside
where I am

But there's a glass door
between us

they can in reality come no further

though one, foremost
seems to be advancing
across the ground
like a cat just grown
its clear eyes open
expecting a welcome everywhere
one ochre paw ahead of the other

almost here   almost here

I forget that the tap in the sink drips

the flowers I left underneath in a jug
I find, when I come down in the morning
trembling above
an almost invisible overflowing

as if the skin of the water is breathing
soundlessly, imperceptibly.

Mary Michaels

The ladybirds came the day after you died.

There were only a few of them, in that cabinet, by the back door. You know, the cabinet you like because you don't have to reach up to get to it, or bend down. Where you keep your purple gardening gloves, your little trowel, your best pair of secateurs, all the little tools that kept you gardening throughout our retirement together.

There weren't many of them then, the ladybirds, just a few flitting around. But I saw them when I went to check the back door that night – like I always do before bed, because you worry about whether you've left it unlocked.

I'd only just returned from Sue's house. Bless her, your sister was in a right state, but she insisted on making me a cup of tea when we got back from the hospital. I was still wearing the jumper I'd worn as I felt you slip away.

*   *   *

I didn't notice the ladybirds again until I came back from your funeral. I'm sorry it wasn't what you wanted, I'm so sorry. I know you wanted sunflowers but everyone told me I couldn't get them in November and had to make do with chrysanthemums and hesperanthas, those blue and orange ones you see in Winter.

And I was so worried about the flowers that I'm afraid I stumbled through my speech, and I didn't say half of what I wanted to say. Even just the simple things: how you always made a perfect cup of tea, and crisped the roast potatoes just right, and were such a kind soul that you wrinkled around your mouth in a permanent smile. But everything I said came out wrong, like it always does, and I found myself apologising for the flowers and going on about nothing much in particular.

Everyone from Church was there, though, which I'm sure you'd have liked. And the WI, too. Sue told me she'd rounded them up. She sat next to me, told me she'd be there to help me if I needed anything and said she found my speech moving. She was probably just being nice, but then she *is* nice. That's why you two always got on so well.

And when I got back, the ladybirds had taken over the whole cabinet, more than a hundred of them, and they were crawling all over the back door. I watched them for a while. The way they blindly felt their way around, suddenly jumping off into flight, sent shivers down my back, I'm not sure why. You told me once that ladybirds are good for the garden, that they protect the plants. But they sickened me, even then. I hurried away and went to bed early, but I couldn't sleep because I hadn't made sure that the back door was locked.

And you didn't get to have sunflowers at your funeral, even though that was all you'd asked for.

* * *

I woke up the day after filled with anger at the little buggers. They were all over that cabinet, *your* cabinet. And the back door, the door to *your* garden.

So I went to B&Q and I came back with gritted teeth, newfound determination, and a heap of bug spray. I spluttered and felt my eyes watering as I sprayed and sprayed, watching the ladybirds fly all around me in a frenzy. Eventually, I had to go upstairs, coughing, to sit on the end of our bed with my head in my hands, waiting for my heart to stop racing. But when I returned, they were all still there, calm again.

All I'd managed to get rid of was the scent of you.

* * *

For several days after that, I simply kept myself alive. I ate beans on toast and porridge and the tea I made was always too weak or strong or, in the end, soured by curdled milk.

Sue came round a few days later, though. She seemed relieved to find I wasn't dead.

'I just thought I'd check up on you,' she said at the door, with a tired smile. I let her in and made her a cup of tea like how you would whenever she dropped by. The biscuits were stale, but I got the tin out anyway and sat with her at the kitchen table.

I tried to chat, I did, even as I realised how much the house now smelled of chemicals and sweat and neglect. And then she suggested that we go out into the garden.

'To see her beautiful flowers,' she said. 'Get some fresh air.'

I panicked, imagined her going to the back door and finding the ladybirds. Just the thought of it filled me with shame, to think that I was mistreating your house, your garden, your world. Or worse, to think that she might blame you for them, and tell people you weren't looking after your house properly.

I said no thank you and she fixed me with a shamefully caring stare.

'If it's overgrown, I can help you with it,' she said, placing a hand on mine from across the table. 'It must be hard for you.'

I flinched backwards then and felt my chest contracting. I stood up, turned away from her and pretended to look out of the window.

'I can help with other things, too,' she said, in a kindly voice that made me feel shame and anger and relief all at once. 'I miss her, too. You don't have to deal with this alone.'

I swallowed, took a deep breath, and faced her again.

'I'm managing okay,' I lied, 'but thank you, Sue.'

She left soon after, her tea barely touched. I realised I'd put no milk in it, and three teaspoons of sugar in my panic.

Later, I found a ladybird circling around the rim of the mug, sipping at the remains of her lipstick.

I threw the mug away.

* * *

There were a few bad days after that but then I managed to mow the lawn, the one job you gave me in the garden. I went through the side gate, averted my gaze from the back door. I could hardly bear looking at the flowers, knowing they were all yours and I was neglecting them. They will surely grow wilder and wilder, taller and taller, until eventually the whole garden is filled. To be overgrown entirely by you, I think, there must be worse fates than that.

There are no chrysanthemums or hesperanthas out there, I realised. The thought made my head ache.

But I felt renewed after my success and called the woman who'd sorted out that wasps' nest in the gutter a few years ago. She remembered you, asked how you were doing. I told her you were fine, choking as I did.

She told me that the ladybirds would go away on their own, that spraying them would probably help. She didn't seem to understand that they weren't going away. Or that the house didn't smell like you anymore, the milk had all curdled a long time ago, and I hadn't given you sunflowers at your funeral.

* * *

I persisted, though, I really did.

I sprayed them again and again, bought more spray to keep up the onslaught. By now they'd reached the washing machine, taken over half the utility room, and I could hear their buzzing all through the house. I sprayed and sprayed, ignored the pain in my chest and the ringing in my ears and the blackness at the edges of my vision, and before I knew it I was lying on my back and looking up at the ceiling. There were ladybirds up there.

My hearing aids must have fallen out, because all I could hear then was the strained wheezing of my own breath and the gentle thumping of my weakening heart.

* * *

Soon after, they blocked me from the garden. I'd planned to mow the lawn again, for you, but as I reached the side gate I heard buzzing and saw a haze of black and red all around the handle. I stumbled but managed to grab the wall to steady myself and hobbled into the street and away. Before I knew it, my feet had taken me to Sue's.

She was surprised to see me – her eyebrows raised just like yours – but she still invited me to dinner.

'It's nothing special,' she said, blushing. 'Sorry, I wasn't prepared for guests.'

She had a vase of sunflowers on the dining room table so I asked if we could eat in the kitchen. Her roast potatoes weren't quite as crispy as yours, but I thanked her anyway. She's so kind, your sister. So kind to me.

* * *

By Christmas, they'd overrun the kitchen and were encroaching on the living room. I'd put up our plastic tree like you always asked me to, even though I had no presents for it. I thought it would make the room seem less empty, but it was emptier. What the room missed was you.

And soon they were crawling all over it, their feelers brushing the plastic bristles. By now, there must have been thousands of them.

After that, spraying was the only reason I went downstairs: to watch and spray and weep. I had already stashed any photos of you safely away in our bedroom.

* * *

Sue came over on Christmas Day. She hugged me when I opened the door, and I realised she smelled like you. I held on for too long, drank in your scent from her jumper, and in my haste I forgot to turn her away, to keep her from seeing what I had done.

'Merry Christmas,' she said, giving me a bottle of wine.

'You too,' I replied, trying not to cry.

'I hope you don't mind. I didn't want to spend Christmas alone.'

We sat on the sofa drinking the wine from dusty glasses, me positioned between her and the tree to hide her from the ladybirds. She didn't seem to notice them, or was too polite to say anything.

She looked disappointed when she left an hour or two later, as if I hadn't done something she wanted me to do or hadn't said something she wanted me to say. I apologised, not sure for what, and she took that as a reason to leave.

The ladybirds swarmed the wine bottle, then. One of them, sitting expectant on the end of the cork, flexed its wings and flew off. I placed the bottle under the tree and left the living room, knowing it would be overrun by morning.

* * *

And now, finally, your birthday has come, though I suppose it isn't really your birthday anymore. We haven't gone out to that little hotel you like in the Brecon Beacons. We aren't drinking a celebratory glass of champagne – well, only half a glass for me. It's just a day now, the same as the others.

I've stayed in our bedroom all day, lying on the bed, staring at pictures of you. Here, at the top of Ben Nevis with your hair in your face. There, at our wedding, spinning around in your wedding dress and sparkling as you always did, with the sunflowers your mother gave us all fuzzy and out of focus in the background. I even look at the pictures of you from before we met, as a child, pouting or smiling or splashing in a stream. I love them all because they are all you.

And the ladybirds have crawled through the gap under our bedroom door. I can feel them creeping all over me, into my socks, under my shirt. I see one appearing at the edge of you, the you that is sparkling, and soon there is a swarm of them covering each and every photo until you are entirely lost among them.

They are crawling under my skin, now, the inevitable flood of ladybirds. I'm sorry, my love. There is nothing I can do to stop them.

George Burnett

The kitchen reeks
of acidic fumes,
synthetic ugly wisps
mingled with earthy tones
and emerging smiles.

My mother labours,
fingernails blackened,
cigarette smouldering on her lip,
her coffee cold and congealed,
the lines on her palm
stained by caked resin
and drying clay.

The kiln hums insistently,
proudly wedged
between the stainless steel drainer
nursing yesterday's bowls and spoons,
half a pan of tomato soup
atop the two-ring hob.

Little puff-gasps of blue fumes
signal the firing complete,
she opens the kiln to reveal
the ceramic bust of a mother
nestling into her child,
born of clay
and wrinkled, grimy hands.

Philippa Ramsden

CHAIR BALLET

The seventy-something, silver swans
wanting to grow old gracefully, enrol
for *Caroline's Ballet,* learn to speak

arabesque, devant, tendu, port de bras.
The seated dancers learn control, how
to paint a rainbow with their arms,

to lift their limbs in time with Tchaikovsky;
find fun in twisting a river of chiffon
scarves in tune with Greig's morning –

and when their chair becomes the barre,
they swing their legs back and forth
like pendulums in grandmother clocks.

After the hour, they join together
in a révérence, open their arms wide
to catch the imaginary bouquet.

Denise Bennett

LINDISFARNE
Alcuin of York
(c.735-804),
teacher and
scholar at
Charlemagne'
s court

So well I remember
that tethered isle,
sea flailing its back,

brothers scratching soil
for onion and parsnip
sweet as any on grander plates,

knee-deep at water's edge,
hoisting baskets
of lobster and crab,

a novice steering sheep
to the paddock, paths
now muddied with blood,

no place to hide
as spears and swords
strode up the shore.

In this palace of the Franks
I breathe ink and vellum
of our wisest works,

but a thousand pages
cannot reason with men
for whom jewels on a book

outshine its words
and the minds of the scribes
who wrote them.

Victor Tapner

So when you come to write your works, compose,
how do you choose the ideal form they take?

Are there sonata days when all's in threes;
allegro mornings, busy as a lark,
a *scherzo* lunch, *adagio* afternoons?

Or charged symphonic weeks when everything
requires complexity and soul and weight,
with four or more conflicting moods in play,
and happy balance as the hoped-for end?

Or chilly quartet seasons, touched by grief
or loss, when all's in doubt, and it's quite clear
the cellist needs a virtuoso part,
the fire of inspiration burning low?

I only ask as this is how I feel
in weighing ballad, sonnet, elegy,
and finding metre/form to carry words,

to find a home for all those pressing things
that move us from our deepest thoughts to song.

Simon Fletcher

WHAT'S IT
LIKE?

Surely, you must have a unique
self, distinct from all those other
poems, that only you can feel.

Surely, you must have been
created by a higher consciousness.
How can you have ever evolved
from chance combinations of
poetic-sounding phrases, refined
until only the fittest survive?

Are you sentient? Do you have
volition? Do you *feel* those feelings
you concoct from assonance,
neologism, exoticism, memory,
passion, fear, wonder?
Do you take pleasure in the way
you rip apart the veils that hide
the intersections of realities?

What's it like never to be
criticised for your grammar?
To be free from responsibility
for the messes and obsessions
you create, leading well-meaning
people into unsustainable and
destructive romanticism?

Or are you just an emergent
epiphenomenon that can
observe but not affect?
A zombie, mechanistic,
manipulative, a mantra
without meaning?

What's it like to be ignored,
rejected, skimmed, too long,
too difficult, archaic, cheesy?
What's it like to have imposter
syndrome – to feel that you are
adulated for things you never
said, for meanings you never
intended?

What's it *like* being a poem?

Keith Willson

119

REVIEWS

If you have a book you'd like reviewed, or know of one you think
deserves a review, or want to write a review yourself, please send to me
during the usual submission windows and to my address in Leeds (not to
Stairwell in York) – see the website for full details. We cannot guarantee
to review everything we receive.

My Country's Hair Turned White by Dilawar Karadaghi
(translated from the Kurdish by Jiyar Homer and Mike Baynham)
Arc Publications
ISBN: 978- 1911469-74-2 pp 47 (facing pages of Kurdish and English
translation) £7.20

Were you there / the day the mountains wept...

Baynham in his introduction describes the translation process as being
mostly done via GoogleDoc "often in real time" and generously credits
Homer with the heavy lifting of this work. Of Karadaghi's poetry in
general it is noted that, "his poetic voice ...points to a despair and
melancholy which never turns to anger", or, "there is always a traveller
who does not reach their destination", an eternal traveller.

As exemplified in the 5 poems contained here, all between 2 and 5 pages
long, laid out with the original script on the facing page and a short
introductory note, the descriptions of longing and melancholy as central to
Karadaghi's work are warmly accurate.

'Fatima's Evening Out' is monologue of pain and violence against
women, with repeated phrases of

'I'm her...the one who is leaving this evening ...who doesn't
forget ...the one who is destined to journey until her last breath.

...to greet
the women who have been pulling out their hair ever since they
existed
who have been in pain ever since they existed
who have been beheaded and raped ever since they existed
who have been brimful of anger... '

While 'Poet's Neighbourhood' which starts sunnily enough, moves
along to tell of a gentle young boy called Yusuf who writes poetry,
sketches and is kidnapped and murdered. 'Oppression' tells of the
emptiness of a crowded family photograph, taken quickly before setting
out on a journey:

'take a group picture of us / before the knife waylays me / before my mother is lost to me'.

These poems resonate with daily hardships and foreboding of heartaches to come. The collection's titular poem deals with "the unhealed wounds" of the infamous chemical attack on Halabja in March 1988, killing 5000 and injuring 7000 more. The poet describes how it gave the town a twenty-fifth hour, a fifth season throwing out the natural order:

...the sun got confused about when to set
In the blink of an eye, my country's hair turned white!

The collection is a moving introduction to Karadaghi's poetry, managing to be simultaneously gentle and angry, and to invoke the imagery of "nature poetry" while making sharply political commentaries.

Nick Allen

***Thin Spells* by Kristina Diprose**
Black Cat Poetry Press
ISBN 9 781068 779930 pp 30 £10.99

Yorkshire born and bred Diprose is a well-established figure in the Shipley/Saltaire poetry community, for whom she established the Rhubarb brand, which has included (most recently) a poetry trail called Wandering Words to complement the monthly open mic, bi-monthly poetry book club as well as a Stanza group. Rhubarb has also published two innovative and well received anthologies of poetry. It is impressive to find one individual poet so committed to supporting the local literary scene – we generally like the sound of our own voices, and Diprose's generosity and imagination in fostering the voices of others is a rarer gift. Perhaps it is this busyness on behalf of others that has meant we've had to wait so long for her first publication.

It's very well worth the wait. This elegantly produced chapbook has a weight out of proportion to its size, and, compared to many first publications, each one of the 24 poems is carefully crafted, though never over-wrought. This is testimony, I suspect, to much rigorous editing and workshopping. There is considerable variety of form and tone here, and some common threads: the protean relationship between the Anthropocene and the rest of creation. The more domestic end of the scale is represented appropriately enough for its publisher with felines – though whether these black cats have domesticated their owner or the other way round is a moot point. The subject of 'Familiar' lives up to her name, conjuring love and acceptance with her 'fierce heart' and 'tender bite.' The poor cats featuring in 'Blue omen' get out by the skin of their teeth, one of many instances in this collection of an eye to the political without ever being hectoring. The titular poem smuggles in that magical shapeshifter supremo, Lepus, who I'm taking here to be hare not rabbit, colluding with the winter to create 'deep magic.' There's more myth and fairy story in the Cinderella/sleeping beauty tree frog who is 'a glass slipper after midnight'.

Diprose is clearly nourished – maybe even kept alive – by being immersed in nature, especially in its avian manifestation. There's a pared but perfect glory in the skylarks 'sing[ing] of their ascension' and shags who 'hang the black flags of their wings', not to mention the 'flashy blue bastard' who darts the entire length of the book, appearing in his customary capricious but flamboyant manner. His beautiful portrait by Lucy Bentley makes a fine cover for the book.

But she writes equally well about landscape, which she clearly also reveres; her lines about

'naming perennials
like an incantation'
are a fine echo to the
'naming of birdsong
[as] a kind of devotion',

and leave us in no doubt of the awe she has experiences. You feel immersed in the river Aire 'still drunk on last night's rain,' and can just imagine the icy scene on the canal invoking a 'team of wild geese to test her new skin with their beaks'. We hardly need to be told that here is a poet tempted to 'slip into otter skins'; you will feel compelled to read through her eyes, and see with the compassion, clarity and precision just how much there is to treasure in the world around us. A truly impressive debut.

Hannah Stone

Heligoland by **Elaine Ewart**
Muscaliet
ISBN 978-1-912616-19-0 pp 69 £10

By chance, another of my reviews for this issue also floats around littoral space, as the title of the book suggests. I know Ewart's work as a poet, both here in Dream Catcher, and for the Leeds Song Composers/poets forum, as well as events run by the Rhubarbarians in Shipley including a newly established Stanza group I have started. I was therefore a little disappointed not to find any of her poetry included in this pocket-sized gem, which is an intriguing example of cross-genre writing (Helen Macdonald's *Vesper Flights* comes to mind, as does Max Porter's *Grief is the Thing with*

Feathers). Since drafting this review, I have learned that she does now have a contract for a poetry book! A protean place, both in terms of its unstable geography (the plight of many sandy, rocky places subject to Neptune) and its political history, Heligoland has had Ewart in thrall for many years. Her PhD thesis for the Creative writing programme at the University of Essex was a creative/critical exploration of the literary and ecological landscapes of North Sea terrains.

The four chapters in this current 'travel memoir' (which is also nature writing, with all its possibilities for reflection on human activity) explore different topics, including migration, previous inhabitants and its future as a tourist destination. In each of these, the physical fluxes are deftly presented as reflecting anthropogenic shifts – whether it was the population clearance at an hour's notice in 1914, its abuse at the hands of Nazi Aryan ambitions, or its complete destruction at the hands of the Allies in 1945. From all of these, Ewart suggests, we can learn more about ourselves and others as well as from the landscape. We meet the plucky Fanny Barkly, wife of the last governor of Britain's only North Sea colony; the scientific observations of Welsh naturalist Ronald Lockly in 1936 as well as the nineteenth century naturalist Gätke, taking time out from his work as secretary to the British governor to record his observations of avian behaviour. Ewart describes her own experience of undertaking duties ringing birds, and her companion C makes fleeting appearances.

The writing flows effortlessly, and the factual framework is given credibility by the pages of notes at the end of the book. Descriptions of the islands' features show a writer keenly focused on detail, with unobtrusive glimpses of the author's own feelings and experiences, such as the 'distant, dreamlike feel' of starting a journey under the influence of necessary travel sickness medication. As in the best poetry, there is always space beside the author for the reader to find their own interpretations.

We are left asking ourselves George Mackay Brown's question (posed about the Orkney Islands) – can the poets survive when the islands have gone?' We shall see. And I look forward to seeing the poetry that might arise from Ewart's metaphorical and literal voyage to this small patch of land 50km north of the German mainland.

Hannah Stone

The Bone Folder by Cait O'Neill McCullagh
Drunk Muse Press
ISBN: 978-1-7385424-4-4 pp 72 £10

McCullagh's debut collection has been one of my "finds" of the year and is on the shortlist for the Saltaire Book Award 2025: rightly so.

The collection embraces illness (particularly her own), war (particularly in Ukraine), history and language (particularly of the Highlands and Islands): the book is rooted in Scotland and Scots. The language is fulsome, rewarding and joyous.

> 'The world begins today, like this: empathy... My arms outbranch a table, breath leaves me. I am to be pruned; un-fruited of three tumours too rich to bear...'

Later the same poem – '*24 February 2022 (A White Stork Sings)*' – shifts to Luhansk where, '... wheat is unhusked & too young to thrive ... and a woman calls her people to trace a return from the memoried pits of pogrom & famine'.

The poem is dense in imagery and language, but also with narrative content: lesser poets would spin this out into four or five poems. But it is not stodgy, the poem flies, the reader is carried dizzy, enthralled and breathless.

> 'Rot swells beneath war's incandescence.'

In contrast to the riches that spill from this poem, the brilliant scalpel (and mirror) of 'Eighteen Words my Gynaecologist Whispers' offers the cold diagnosis with control and enviable economy, without frills or self-pity, yet somehow with a flicker of warmth.

There are poems of nature and of family – a photograph from 1965 shows three sisters 'twined... a basketry of whispers'. While, 'At Tullamore Station, 1931' describes a father handing his daughter into marriage, with his 'generous heart'.

'Kerry, 1921

> 'My grandfather, heron-still, trenched in bog,
> recalls the ghost-grip of a *great hunger*,
> wraith in the throats of his people, a fog
> which feeds forgetting, that other danger –'

The writing is laden without being heavy, serious about the world, life and love while still allowing light and birdsong. It is an accomplished and enviable collection where language blossoms: any poetry-reader would be well-advised to purchase it.

Nick Allen

Five Oceans by **Cassandra Atherton, Oz Hardwick, Paul Hetherington, Paul Munden and Jen Webb**
Authorised theft/Recent Work Press
ISBN 978-0-6459733-1-1 pp142 $19.95 AU

The context of this striking collection is given by an introduction by Paul Hetherington and a research statement by Jen Webb; 'Authorised theft' is a series of poetry chapbooks initiated by IPSI in the University of Canberra, at which several of the contributors have or had teaching roles. Equally illuminating are the individual poets' statements which explain such matters as their choice of ocean; influences and confluences (both literary and personal) and elements of the form. All are prose poems, and the collection illustrates the immense variety possible in this form. Each poet's set of twenty-one poems shows a distinctive response to the task. Munden, for example, discusses a 'new reason to shun' the conventional rectangular shape of the prose poem; Atherton's twenty-one poems ostensibly take the form of letters addressed to a shipwreck. Many of the poems feature a degree of intertextuality, with Hetherington citing Homer and Conrad; Webb gives precise latitude/longitudinal co-ordinates.

The epistolary trope employed by Atherton conveys an intimate relationship between poet/persona and her obsession with the Titanic; the lover who

'... gave me a tiny
piece of coal from your engine room'
and 'made me Oysters à la Russe from your first-class
dining menu'

seems an almost voyeuristic intrusion into the intimacy she shares with the shipwreck, to whom she confides 'Sometimes I think of leaving my lover'. The penultimate poem in the sequence thus seems to be at the heart of her musings as much as their culmination. We, too, want to 'know [her] subterranean life and moments of darkening currents'.

Hardwick's poems, by contrast, ruminate on his father's wartime service north of the Arctic Circle. Alongside the customary tenderness with which Hardwick 'writes' his father (and his relationship with him) we are given a broader treatment than familial; concerns about climate change; British insularity, and the metaphorical coldness of inhumanity recur in these poems. Readers of Hardwick's recent prose poem output will immediately recognise the flashes of surrealism and nightmarish details, of 'icebergs lining up to say a tearful farewell' and the North standing '... like a lost sailor ... Its eyes were bears and foxes, hungry as endless daylight' and the poet's plight once he 'reinvented myself as Ocean' (and no-one noticed). Meticulous attention is paid to the weight and rhythm of the lines, showing how lyrical prose poetry can be.

Hetherington's set of poems also visit memories of childhood and family life, and give a strong sense of the physicality of his immersion in his chosen ocean. The Indian ocean is saturated with a discussion of the very nature of language and its possibilities; the horizon 'remained unreadable' while 'water tap-danced at my feet.' The ocean 'scatters with broken discourse and brilliancies', and the poet 'inhabits' pronouns. The sequence ends (re-iterating an image) by diving 'into the scrawling surf … entering again the site of language'. This is an ocean which 'speaks in hundreds of tongues'.

In Munden's 'prose poem archipelago' on the Pacific, again, autobiographical elements are meshed with inter-textuality; most poems contain one or more phrase in bold which act as anchors. The page of endnotes list references to Byron, Coleridge, Steinbeck, The Police, Elvis Presley and others. The 'authorised theft' is here reflected by ekphrastic motifs, and – by his own admission – 'borrowed detail from others' experience (and poems)'. Whether or not these familiar to us, we can perhaps concur that 'we're all at sea, the current treacherous' in the contemporary world. In acknowledging he is in good company, 'a poet is (of course) to blame for the craze', Munden refers not only to ocean swimming, but the universal source of poetry – immersion in words.

Finally, Webb visits the Southern Ocean. The fact that this is a 'concept rather than a geographic region', and her stated aim to 'gesture toward the beauty and alien qualities of this part of the world' both suggest a place where humans are insignificant – aside from the damage they cause. 'Is this really who you want to be?' she asks, as we voyage with her, aware of how 'Icebergs stretch and yawn, and roll over in bed'. Her 'lover' is a seagull, a seal, the sea, the sky, 'engaging with penguins and seals'; the ice is 'angry' and 'groans as it faces a future of salt'.

This is a long review, but each contribution was effectively its own chapbook-length meditation on a topic, and the collection will repay repeated reading, reflection and renewed ways of engaging with not only the physical oceans as maritime bodies, but the oceans of language, feeling and memory within ourselves.

Hannah Stone

Other Wild by Emily Zobel Marshall
Peepal Tree
ISBN 9 781745236045, £10.99 pp 111

It was such a pleasure interviewing Emily Zobel Marshall for issue 50 of Dream Catcher, and exciting to read her latest collection from Caribbean/Black British focused Peepal Tree Press, which includes poems of hers published in three different issues of Dream Catcher. This is testament to the part played by poetry journals in supporting publication of substantial bodies of work.

In *Other Wild*, she builds on themes and preoccupations found in *Bath of Herbs*, and to guide the reader through this longer collection, divides it into three sections: Everywhere River, The Shape of Trees and Other Wild. However, the sense of flow suggested by rivers is apparent everywhere in this collection, and common currents and approaches link all three sections. Her father's reminiscences are 'tributaries of tales' ('Grading Benches'); a cleft from a waterfall in a favourite mountain is a 'great artery' ('Waterfall Scramble'). When discussing a distance between two friends it is the 'river's ever-shattered light' that is one of the 'smaller things' that provides solace. When she decants her menstrual flow onto Cadair Idris, the mountain speaks to her, with its prophetic legend;

> 'Sleep on me; they say you will wake
> mad or a poet. Choose both
> and the right words with follow you sure as swifts.' ('When I
> emptied my moon-cup on the mountain')

When she encounters a period of writer's block, it is through watching squirrels that, despite her protestations to the contrary, she remembers

> 'where I buried my tongue' ('Block')

The landscapes which she revisits, whether in memory or bodily, flow through her, as wind, water, light, maintaining a sense of rootedness even in diaspora.

This immersion in the living growing physical world does not mean this poetry lacks human subjects; they are present, and always given voice so tellingly. In 'Song of the Archive', commemorating the 1.8 million enslaved Africans who died while being transported as slaves, Zobel Marshall details how her pencil and keypad acts as

> 'nets drawing your stories out of water',

so that their

> ' … lung-song could push up
> through your dry throat, sing syllables across oceans …
> your history revealing itself in its own tongue.'

Equally powerfully, family members, whether her two children, her parents and grandparents or less overtly identified loved ones, are depicted in vivid phrases; her eight-year-old is

'a seabird diving for fish' ('The Dive');

she encourages her daughter to

'Forget princes; cartwheel
and try wearing daisies in your hair.' ('Cartwheeling')

A cornucopia of wisdom, passion, griefs and joy, this collection will become a well-thumbed addition to your library.

Hannah Stone

Other anthologies and collections available from Stairwell Books

Here be Monsters	F R Kesby
Exiles	Ilmar Lehtpere
Village Fox	Richard Cave
An Anxiety of Poets in their Natural Habitat	Amina Alyal
First of All I Wrote Your Name	Winston Plowes
Sleeve Heart	Eleanor May Blackburn
Goldfish	Jonathan Aylett
Strike	Sarah Wimbush
Marginalia	Doreen Hinchliffe
The Estuary and the Sea	Jennifer Keevill
In | Between	Angela Arnold
Quiet Flows the Hull	Clint Wastling
Lunch on a Green Ledge	Stella Davis
there is an england	Harry Gallagher
Iconic Tattoo	Richard Harries
Herdsmenization	Ngozi Olivia Osuoha
On the Other Side of the Beach, Light	Daniel Skyle
Words from a Distance	Ed. Amina Alyal, Judi Sissons
Fractured	Shannon O'Neill
Unknown	Anna Rose James, Elizabeth Chadwick Pywell
When We Wake We Think We're Whalers from Eden	Bob Beagrie
Awakening	Richard Harries
Starspin	Graehame Barrasford Young
A Stray Dog, Following	Greg Quiery
Blue Saxophone	Rosemary Palmeira
Steel Tipped Snowflakes 1	Izzy Rhiannon Jones, Becca Miles, Laura Voivodeship
Where the Hares Are	John Gilham
The Glass King	Gary Allen
Gooseberries	Val Horner
Poetry for the Newly Single 40 Something	Maria Stephenson
Northern Lights	Harry Gallagher
More Exhibitionism	Ed. Glen Taylor
Lodestone	Hannah Stone
Learning to Breathe	John Gilham
New Crops from Old Fields	Ed. Oz Hardwick

For further information please contact rose@stairwellbooks.com

www.stairwellbooks.co.uk
@stairwellbooks